Speak Out, Black Sisters

Awa Thiam

Speak Out, Black Sisters

Feminism and Oppression in Black Africa

Translated by Dorothy S. Blair

Pluto  Press

This edition first published 1986 by Pluto Press
345 Archway Road, London N6 5AA
and 141 Old Bedford Road,
Concord, MA 01742, USA
Reprinted 1991

First published in 1978 by Editions Denoël as
La Parole aux Négresses.

British Library Cataloguing in Publication Data
Thiam, Awa
   Speak out, Black sisters, feminism and oppression
   in Black Africa.
   1. Muslims, Black – Africa   2. Women, Muslim –
   Africa   3. Sex discrimination against Women –
   Africa
   I. Title   II. La parole aux negresses. *English*
305.4'862977'06   HQ1170

ISBN 0 7453 0050 2

Printed in Great Britain
by Billing and Sons Ltd, Worcester

Contents

As may be a drop of water in the ocean, or yet a teardrop
    in the sea,
WE MUST
proclaim out loud what all women murmur in thought
denounce the crimes committed against women, mutilations
    that women
endure with resignation
offer resistance at every level
    active resistance
    effective resistance
to all oppression
whatever its source – unremitting
Only by countless voices in unison,
only by countless acts of resistance,
the countless sum of desires for change,
a limitless sum of goodwill
    will to change the nature of our lives, could we change the
present face of the world
    and straight away, the status of woman could end the
oppression and monstrous exploitation endured by women,
oppression and exploitation which were, and still are, in our
day, the daily lot of women. Strength will reside solely in the
multitude of voices, of people, of consciences resolved to
effect a radical change in all the present decadent social
structures. There is no other way.

There is no compromise between liberty and slavery
                                            Patrice Lumumba

Acknowledgements

I wish to thank:

my father for the widespread research he undertook for me into the origin of excision and infibulation, not only in the Koran and the Hadiths, but also in diverse Arab texts;

my mother for the encouragement she gave me to do this work and for facilitating my contacts with certain women;

my uncles, aunts, cousins of both sexes in Guinea and Mali, my brothers and sisters in Ghana, Nigeria and Ivory Coast, who helped me — on many different levels — in my research;

all the women who confided in me.

To my family, to whom I owe everything
To my sisters and brothers – throughout the world – who are struggling for the abolition of sexism patriarchy and every form of domination of man by man.
To the Amazons of Africa, America and Bohemia
To the anti-sexist warrior women of all times
To Zingha
To Claude Imbert and Elisabeth De Fontenay
To El Hadj Seydou Nourou Tall

Preface

I would like to say a few words about Awa Thiam's book, not in my capacity as a writer; even less in the name of what we call the values of our Western civilization. It is not as a feminist either, that I speak; it is quite simply as a woman.

It is no longer essential to be a feminist in order to be conscious of the universal oppression experienced by women past and present, oppression which takes many different forms, from the most refined to the most vicious, the most visible burdens not always being the most serious. In Europe, mass burning of witches took place from the fourteenth to the seventeenth century, because their parallel power threatened that of men and of the Church; in China there was the mutilation of girls' feet to prevent them literally, as well as metaphorically, from running around, a tradition which was perpetuated for nearly a thousand years, until the coming of Mao Tse-Tung; in the Middle East, countless women are deprived of all rights, all education, and kept in confinement from puberty to menopause; these familiar examples are only the most striking forms of control exercised over the bodies and minds of women.

In diverse countries, men have denounced repression and abuses of power. But, curiously enough, when these are applied to women – second-class citizens – a modest veil is cast over reality. It is as if injustices suffered by women had nothing to do with oppression in general, but merely expressed the way every race has of putting women 'in their place' in society. Now justice never drops from heaven. Never have the privileged, the powerful – be they so as the result of fortune, birth, sex or the colour of their skin – spontaneously shared their privileges. Every liberty, every right, has had to be fought for. In many countries women have not yet begun this struggle. For, in order to win independence, one must first be conscious of one's dependence. And that is probably the most difficult stage.

The case histories and experiences which you are about to read, do not constitute a manifesto, nor do they express rebellion. They make no claims. They are the quite unpretentious confidences which Awa Thiam has managed to collect in all their simplicity, sometimes in all their awkwardness, their pathos deriving from a resignation to destiny which is considered inherent in women's condition. The author has not tried to bring us scientific information or statistics. Others have already done this. She brings us something rarer, something missing up till now: life itself, not as seen by an observer, but as it is experienced by the woman herself.

The Black women who express themselves here are not conscious of injustice and have not yet discovered solidarity and hope. Each one speaks for herself, isolated in her family cell, without information about what goes on in the rest of the world. The lives that they live are, in their eyes, the normal condition of women. But although for centuries they have been kept apart from all decision-making, reduced to their reproductive functions and tied to domestic and agricultural toil, the fact that they are beginning to speak out is a sign of their growing awareness. This awareness will deepen and broaden. But it was important for someone – in particular, a woman – to decide to lift the taboo, to break the silence.

These women from Mali, Senegal and Guinea, tell the stories of their childhood, subjected as they were to the authority of father, brothers or marabout (Muslim teacher or holy man); then of their lives subjected to the authority of the husband. They tell what it means to live with polygamy, what love can imply when a woman shares a husband with two, three or twenty co-wives. Some of these women have agreed to speak for the first time of the taboo subject, excision, and to tell their experiences of this mutilation, which is presented to them as 'essential for the enhancement of their femininity, by suppressing the useless vestiges of the phallus', and which permits them to become 'more docile spouses and more fertile mothers'.

For the first time, Black women who are not members of any official organization, not committed to any doctrine, describe for us the reality of their daily existence, seen from their own level. The great merit of this book is that it finally allows the silent women of history to speak out.

They speak, but they do not accuse. For, in these countries where religious and family traditions are implacable, revolt would be tantamount to social suicide. To refuse excision or infibulation – even supposing this were possible at the age when these operations are carried out – would mean condemning one-self to become a voluntary outcast from society. As a Sudanese man writes, 'women with gaping holes don't find any takers in our country'.

So, what steps must be taken? Spreading information – but this information must come from women themselves. They themselves must break the curse of silence, for anthropologists and journalists have always been extremely discreet about this mutilation which they describe as an 'initiation ceremony' or a 'picturesque custom'. Since these tortures are only inflicted on little girls incapable of protesting, they have never waxed indignant over a practice which perpetrates an unnecessary amputation on a human being, doing violence to her biological nature, but which also, (unlike the circumcision of boys) presents serious dangers to her health and irreversible consequences for her full development.

The people of the Third World have been the object of much study. Doctors have fought against infant mortality and endemic diseases. Industrialists, not overburdened with scruples, have applied their attention to the question of raw materials, with familiar results. Only when it is a matter of taking a stance on sexual mutilations, have these scruples emerged, in the name of a sudden respect for local traditions! And so, thanks to the lack of information on the part of some people and the prudent silence of others, a ritual has been maintained that does not even have any religious basis.

Several humanitarian organizations have tried to alert public opinion. In 1972, an American woman founded WIN (Women's International Network) to undertake research and to study the incidence of excision and infibulation – also known as Pharaonic circumcision. These researches proved that they are carried out on MILLIONS of little girls and adolescents in 26 countries of Africa. Medical reports and petitions have been sent to the United Nations and to the World Health Organization (WHO). Without result.

In 1975, the Year of the Woman, the Association *Terre des Hommes*, whose headquarters are in Lausanne, also tried, through press conferences, to make the World Health Organization aware of its responsibilities. But there, too, the reply was that 'ritual operations are the result of social and cultural concepts, the study of which is not the responsibility of WHO'.

Specialists in tropical medicine, African and European gynaecologists and Black midwives have all published reports on the medical effects of these mutilations, especially in childbirth, but these reports have remained confidential. The majority of doctors have claimed to be unaware of the problem. This has frequently been an excuse not to treat women. In the entire Christian world, from antiquity until the middle of the sixteenth century (when Ambroise Paré altered the practice), doctors were forbidden to care for a woman in labour 'to spare her modesty', and obstetrics were excluded from medical manuals 'out of respect for morality'. Even today, the majority of people who have had some knowledge of the tragic consequences of these operations, prefer to keep cautiously clear of any form of fight. This is evidenced by the following letter which exactly reflects the traditional attitude. It is the answer given by a French doctor in Africa to Edmond Kaiser, founder of *Terre des Hommes*:

I beg to acknowledge receipt of your letter in which you ask for any information which I may have regarding the ablation of the clitoris in children, adolescent girls and women, especially in Africa. This is unfortunately a question that I have not attempted to study in detail, simply because the subject is rather delicate and it is difficult, especially for a man, to obtain precise information in this matter.

It is common knowledge that the excision of girls is a generalized custom with Muslims, including Arabs. Among the peoples of Eastern Africa, and in particular among the

Afar and Somalis, there is, in addition to the ablation of the clitoris, a more extensive mutilation of the female sexual organs. As you are aware, this is known as infibulation. I have no information on any comprehensive study of mutilations in the world at large. We know from authors of antiquity (Strabon, etc.) that this type of operation was held in high honour here in olden times. Perhaps what we are witnessing here today is simply a survival of what the ancients noted in former times, proving the enduring nature of such pernicious customs.

The procedures adopted by the old women who carry out these cruel operations differ. In the case of the Afar, they generally remove everything they can, clitoris, hymen, strips of flesh from the labia minora and majora, and, using thorns for sutures, constitute one single narrow aperture, which the young men cannot always succeed in penetrating. For, contrary to the Somalis, who cut open a negotiable passage with a dagger on the wedding night, such 'artificial defloration' is not permitted among the Afar. If, after several days of useless and painful efforts, the fortress resists, the marriage is annulled and the impenetrable woman is sometimes unjustly discredited.

The number of girls who die, the victims of excessive professional zeal on the part of some matriarch, is apparently quite high, although no statistics exist. I had occasion to meet a case of this nature in the course of a journey to Ethiopia. I had just drawn up near a group of Afar huts, when a woman came and asked me to treat two sick little girls. I followed her into a hut and saw two children aged about eight lying naked on mats, next to each other, with a rag covering the middle of their bodies. When I removed this, I realized the nature of their illness. The old woman who had operated on them had cut away so much flesh that the wound had been unable to 'knit'. Their legs were slightly parted to reveal a gaping aperture of eight to ten centimetres in length and two centimetres approximately at the widest point. The cervix was visible in the depths of this cavity. The whole area was swollen and surrounded by abscesses.

I tried to apply dressings, but I could not touch the girls without eliciting screams. When I had cleaned up the 'operational area' as best I could, I sprinkled sulphonamide powder over the abscesses and left a supply of this powder. I could do no more, nor could I evacuate them, in the state they were in, over hundreds of kilometers in a region where there were no roads. They must have died soon afterwards.

When you talk to the people of the country about the barbarous and dangerous nature of this practice, they have no other explanation than that they are carrying out a custom. They sometimes add that they wanted to protect the girls themselves against temptation. As for the women, they are fatalistic and do not think of complaining.

I think that Europeans might have been able slowly to modify this mentality, in those parts of Africa where they held power. Perhaps they only saw the outlandish side of it, or else they had no time to do more ...

In any case, it would not have been possible to impose new behaviour on colonized peoples by authoritarian means. Wherever this was tried tentatively, by missionaries in Abyssinia, by the English in Kenya, the experiments met with failure. Only one country, Sudan, has taken an official stance and declared excision and infibulation illegal. In order that this decree should not remain a dead letter, Sudan has undertaken a patient information campaign in every village, using itinerant groups of midwives and specially trained social workers. It is a long-term undertaking, because it finds itself up against ancestral customs and family structures which, in every country, have always opposed anything which runs the risk of challenging them.

It needs courage and persistence to denounce a situation that dates from so far back that it seems always to have existed. Awa Thiam, like all those who see the light too soon, will meet with incomprehension, prejudice and hostility. She will need the solidarity of all women. Of African women, in the first place, but also of all women involved in a struggle. 'The last colony in the modern world' will not obtain respect for its rights until women learn solidarity. Solidarity with the millions of women who have been excised, sewn up, veiled, repudiated, sequestered, prostituted or sold, throughout the world. And they must be mindful of the fact that every woman who is exploited, mutilated or subjugated, even ten thousand miles away, subjugates and mutilates all the others.

It is possible to develop without losing one's soul. And in this, as in other respects, a society can no longer stifle the aspirations of half of its members. As the anthropologist Germaine Tillion so well expresses it, 'Nowhere in the world is there any misfortune affecting women that does not have its repercussions beyond the feminine condition; when daughters are abased, their fathers are besmirched; what hurts a mother strikes at her sons'.

Awa Thiam's book bears witness to this female misfortune. It shows women beginning to say 'No!', as yet diffidently and often hesitantly. But this is an appeal to which we must listen.

Benoîte Groult

Part I: The Voices of Black Women

Black women have been silent for too long. Are they now beginning to find their voices? Are they claiming the right to speak for themselves? Is it not high time that they discovered their own voices, that – even if they are unused to speaking for themselves – they now take the floor, if only to say that they exist, that they are human beings – something that is not always immediately obvious – and that, as such, they have a right to liberty, respect and dignity?

Have Black women already spoken? Have they already made themselves heard? Yes, sometimes, but always with the blessing of the men. And then, their voices were not the voices of women. They did not EXPRESS the nature of woman. They did not express a woman's struggles, nor her fundamental problems. In former times, African women did have a say when decisions of great importance were to be made. We should remember Zingha, the Amazon warrior woman, the first to offer resistance to Portuguese colonization in Angola in the seventeenth century (see I.B. Kake, *Anne Zingha**) or Aora Poku, Queen of the Baulé.**

Women must assume their own voices – speak out for themselves. It will not be easy, and the ones who up to now have been enjoying all the privileges – the men – and who have been making

---

* Source references are listed in the bibliography on pages 135-6.

** According to legend, Aora Poku, celebrated for her wisdom, led the Baulé people of the Ivory Coast into exile in the early eighteenth century, to save them from marauding neighbouring tribes. She resettled them in a fertile valley across the Comoë River. Legend has it that she was obliged to sacrifice her only son to placate the god of the river, who then miraculously allowed the fugitives to cross the raging torrent. (Translator's note)

use of women's voices, will not give them up easily. As they have begun to realize the extent of women's liberation movements today, they may have some inkling of danger. Be that as it may, men are reacting. They are warning women; they are threatening them. This is what the prime minister of Senegal, Abdou Diouf, said on the first Senegalese Women's Day in March 1972: 'You have refused the temptation to adopt an aggressive, sterile feminism, which sets you up as the envious rivals of men, full of complexes . . .'

Feminism is on trial. It is not surprising that Abdou Diouf sees feminism as something aggressive, but the fact that he sees it as sterile proves that he has understood nothing and/or wishes to understand nothing. Feminism is aggressive, but it is the aggression of revolution. And because it is revolutionary, it cannot be sterile. Decoded, the message of this quotation, which has not actually been stated, is: 'Refuse the temptation of feminism.'

After this injunction, the prime minister of Senegal continued, ' . . . so that you can assume your position nobly as equal partners'. Moral considerations apart, we would like to know what this equality comprises. How is it translated into concrete terms? By the appointment of a few women as deputies, by admitting a tiny minority of women to public office, by the absolute right of husbands to exploit any number of wives, or by polygamy instituted to the detriment of women? By the inequality of educational opportunities (refusal of bursaries to girls and women students, even at university level, whose situation should make this imperative)? UNESCO's figures on the literacy of girls in Black Africa speak for themselves (*Yearbook of statistics*, UNESCO, 1974). Is the peasant woman working in the ricefields of Casamance in Senegal considered as an equal partner by 'her man' or by any other Senegalese male? What does such equality amount to? To men handing over power to women? No! That is not what African women want at the present time. They want a *de facto* equality of rights and duties.

For a long time, African men delighted in doing down their womenfolk, and indeed, they still do so. This campaign must cease. The problems faced by African women have always been dodged, played down in their own communities, both by the governments in power and by reactionary or pseudo-revolutionary intellectuals.

There is no longer any question of accepting excuses for disregarding these problems, least of all the excuse that is most frequently put forward: that the liberation of Black people in general is far and away more important than the liberation of women. At the risk of repeating ourselves, we say that our wish to stand up as a race, with our own specific characteristics, confronting all other races, does not in any way involve brushing aside the problems of the African woman's deplorable situation. We go beyond the racial problem, since we are taking our stance, not only as Black women, African women, but also as members of the human race, without regard for any ethnic considerations. As far as we are concerned, this human race consists of social classes and two categories of individuals: men and women, whose relationship to each other is that of dominating to dominated.

But that is not all. People, or rather men, have often reduced the problem of women to a problem of complementarity. Who defines this complementarity? The men who prescribe it for us. This complementarity has been systematized, giving excuses for all the forms of oppression and exploitation that the patriarchal system imposes on a woman, by virtue of her sex, both in the family and in organized labour. Should this complementarity not only be challenged but also REDEFINED?

Is it not time for Black women to assume the imperative task of speaking out and taking action? Should they not confer upon themselves the right to do this, not impelled or guided by heads of puppet patriarchal governments, but by the urgent desire to end their wretched situation as a force for production and reproduction, overexploited by capital and the patriarchal system?

Time to take the floor in confrontation. Time to take the floor in revolt and say, 'No!'. To give to speech the power of action. Active speech. Subversive speech. ACT, linking theoretical practice with working practice.

But who are these Black women? Much has been written about them and their customs, rarely have authors written about them objectively. Black men who have been granted the possibility of writing about Black Africa, about African civilization, have either completely ignored the Black woman, or, at most, shown little concern for her. When these men did turn their attention to her, it was to praise her, to sing of her beauty, her 'femininity', to set her up as a sexual object, a muse, a mother and drudge; or to analyse her relationship with the White Man or the Black Man and to criticize her, relegating her to the ranks of the primitive savage.

Her praises were sung by the poets of Negritude. She was partially psychoanalysed in her relationship to the Whites and to her fellow-Blacks – by Franz Fanon, for example, the Black psychiatrist from the Caribbean, in *Black Skin, White Masks*. She was abused, condemned and/or misunderstood by colonials, neo-colonials and the majority of her fellow Black men. But what is the use of writing about Black women, if in so doing we do not learn what they are *in reality*? It is up to these women themselves to set the record straight.

In an attempt to apprehend the true existence of the Black woman, and in particular the African woman, for she is the subject matter of this book, we decided to listen to what she has to say in the French-speaking countries of the Ivory Coast, Guinea, Mali and Senegal, and the English-speaking states of Ghana and Nigeria, when she is given an opportunity to speak for herself. Must we understand from this that she does not normally enjoy this possibility? It is a recognized fact that in patriarchal societies the woman may not speak out. Victims of institutionalized polygamy and forced marriages (whether or not the women are excised or infibulated), African women who have no paid work devote themselves, according to their different ethnic groups, to varying forms of agriculture (rice, cotton, millet, groundnuts, etc) and carry out their domestic tasks. These are, at present, extremely onerous. African women do not have at their disposal the domestic appliances available to consumer society which could relieve them of some of the burden of their endless, arduous tasks: grinding millet, preparing *couscous*, collecting firewood, preparing meals, doing the household washing ... The average Black African woman has no cooker, no refrigerator, no electric mixer or grinder or any other household gadget, such as are available in European countries, even to working-class women.

Faced with crushing problems, what are the possibilities of action open to the Black women of Africa?

First of all, we must get rid of the myth that African societies are matriarchal. If people think that having a say in deciding on who the children should marry, organizing the domestic chores, and looking after the household is the same as having power, they are seriously mistaken. It is similarly a mistake to equate a matrilinear society to a matriarchal society. A woman's sole right is to have no rights.

She has no real power, only a pseudo-power. She can act, insofar as she causes no embarrassment to her husband. She can exist, insofar as she does not upset the capitalist system. Thus, any power she may think she possesses is an illusion. The big decisions are the monopoly of the man, and she is not in any way involved in them. In Black Africa the Black man controls not only his own life, but also that of his wife. This is especially the case in Islamic societies, in which 'a woman can only reach paradise through the intermediary of her husband' – in other words, insofar as she has been responsible for the latter's happiness.

Does the African woman concur with this or not? Does she find satisfaction in such a situation? Does she rebel? Does she blindly accept what 'God-the-Husband' decrees? That is what we shall try to find out, by lending an ear to our Black sisters, albeit briefly, in order to get to know them, however slightly, and through them learn a little more about ourselves. Their voices are reported here by way of interviews, of which we have selected the ones which we thought to be the most significant.

Anyone who is expecting feminist diatribes should not read on. Black women from Africa are talking here. They express themselves simply as they reveal their problems. We can deduce from their own words what their actual relationship to men is, what it means to live their daily lives in their communities. Happy and unhappy experiences: Black women's words and woes.

The analysis which follows these testimonies is by no means exhaustive. It is hoped that this study will inspire criticism and suggestions which will be very welcome and a basis for future works.

Yacine

My father was Senegalese, a naturalized Malian. My mother is from Mali. I am 30. I lived with my parents in Senegal until the break-up of the Federation with Mali in 1960. As my father had died, my mother returned to Mali with all her children.

At 18 I was married to a man from the Ivory Coast, who at the time was living temporarily in Bamako (the capital of Mali). My parents had always made all the decisions concerning me, and I had never had any say in my own affairs. That's the way I'd been brought up. My family are blacksmiths. The only time I've ever set foot in a school is when I went to enrol my two eldest children. My husband had a little business, for which he had to travel between Abidjan, Bamako and Ouagadougou (Upper Volta, now Burkina Faso). He finally decided to settle in Abidjan (the capital of the Ivory Coast), where I was obliged to join him. When I arrived in Abidjan we rented one room in the Treichville district, which was mainly inhabited by Wolof-speaking people from Senegal. I tried hard to adapt to this new life which was completely foreign to me. I had to learn to speak the language of the Baulé and Senufo people. On the other hand, I got on perfectly with the members of the 'Senegalese colony' living in the Ivory Coast, seeing that I understood their language.

We had two children, but we still kept the same little room. I began to feel really cramped. After five years of marriage, I was pregnant for the third time. It was during this pregnancy that my husband returned home one night, about eleven o'clock, accompanied by a young woman. 'This is my new wife,' he told me. 'Her name is X . . . You'll have to let us have the bed. For tonight, you can sleep on the mat there in the corner with the two children.' I was flabbergasted. I wondered if I was dreaming. I felt as if the ground was giving way under my feet. I felt as if I was going to faint, and I sat down on the bed. No, I was not dreaming. I had to give up my bed to this newcomer, my rival. 'What a cheek!' I thought, but I didn't say anything. What was I to do? I didn't have time to take it all in. Still half asleep, I spread out a mat and, like a zombie, lay down with the children. I chose to keep quiet and to submit. What else could I do? Rebel? How? By trying to throw this young woman out of my room? By having a row with my husband? By fighting with him? No – if I'd done this I might have endangered the life of the child I was carrying, as well as my own. The important thing for the moment was to preserve these. From that day, my existence took on a completely different direction. Incomprehensible as it may seem, I chose to take a back seat. The 'new bride' did the cooking and laundry for our husband. These are two activities in which most co-wives take pride, if the results are appreciated by their husbands. All I had to do now was to see to my own affairs and look after the children. It was difficult not to get on each other's nerves: a *ménage à trois* with two children in one room. Every night, I had to swallow the insult of being made to witness – in silence – my husband's amorous antics with my co-wife. After a few days, I couldn't stand it any longer and I asked him – although it wouldn't make much difference to the situation – if he would agree to a screen, separating the room into two, so that he and his new wife could be more private when they felt the need. He thought my idea was excellent, but I had to go to the expense of the installation. After that, they got all the benefit from it.

I was in the fifth month of my pregnancy when this so-called co-wife first barged into the room (my room). The four months during which I still had to carry my third child seemed interminable, living as I did in this crazy atmosphere. I had to make the best of a bad job, or at least, I tried to. I knew nobody in this town that I could confide in. I just went on with my household tasks. The few people that I exchanged a word or two with, or with whom I had some sort of acquaintance, didn't seem sufficiently trustworthy for me to risk confiding in them. Nowadays, it frequently happens that a good number of people you talk to or confide in, far from helping you to solve your problems, broadcast them to others, and more often than not laugh at you behind your back. That's why I avoided getting very friendly with anyone in Abidjan, apart from the fact that my social position didn't allow it – friendship supposes a certain reciprocity. What's more, I've never wanted to involve other people in my domestic problems. Not even my mother. Perhaps that was a serious mistake. But I didn't know any different.

After the birth and the baptism of my third child, I made up my mind to go back to Mali and try to find my mother in Bamako if my husband didn't put an end to the impossible life he was inflicting on me. Days passed. There was no change as far as our *ménage à trois* was concerned. Financially, I was basically dependent on my husband. So would I have to rely on him, in order to leave Abidjan? Without saying a word to him or giving him any inkling of what I was doing, I sold the gold jewellery that my father had made for me while he was still alive, to pay for the ticket from Abidjan to Bamako for myself and the children, and to have a little pocket money. Once I was ready to leave, I told my husband of my decision. 'I can't put up with this kind of life any more. Rather than taking a second wife you'd have done better to try to find a solution to the problems of accommodation that the two of us already had with the children, and to look for a second room. Now that there's nothing more between us, I want to go back to my mother in Bamako.' His only reply was a snigger. 'All the better,' he said, thinking it was a joke, since I depended on him financially. From that moment, I reckoned that I had nothing more to say to him. That same day, after lunch, when he had gone back to town for his business, I collected my children's clothes and my own, as well as my cooking utensils. And I left. I travelled by bus. After a long and difficult journey, I reached Bamako. Fatigue and suffering had left their mark on me. My mother couldn't believe her eyes, as she welcomed me tearfully. When I told her what my life with my husband had been like, she couldn't get over it. A few days after my return, my mother received a letter from my husband, asking for news of me. Then I got a letter from him, asking me to go back to live with him in Abidjan. He declared that he still loved me. I didn't answer his letter. Neither did my mother.

Though up till then he had never put in an appearance at my mother's house, he took advantage of the departure of one of his business friends for Bamako, to ask the man to come and see me and my mother. This man had the job of trying to convince my mother that it was my duty to return to my husband, so that she in turn could put pressure on me. For, in Black Africa, when a woman has had a row with her husband and leaves him to go back to her parents, it is understood that he must come and fetch her, if he wants her back. He can also send a relative, a friend or a delegation of people to discuss the disagreement between him and his wife with his parents-in-law. This is what happened in the case of Mr Y . . . , one of whose wives was a friend of mine in Bamako. She had unjustly been accused of adultery, so she left her husband and went back to live with her parents. When she told them of her grievances, she was received with open arms. Her husband sent a delegation to his wife's family, who requested that he come himself. He did so. Although this woman had only stayed six days with her parents, her husband had nevertheless to pay out a high sum (in relation to the cost of living in Mali). This sum, paid to the wife, is symbolic. It puts the stamp on the reconciliation between the three parties: the husband, the wife and the in-laws. It's a way of saying that the couple have no more problems, or rather that the quarrel between them has been settled. It's also a way of encouraging the husband to take more care of his wife, if he wants to keep her.

I had been at my mother's for six months when this gentleman arrived, sent by my husband. From the day I left him with my children, I had never received a penny from him. My mother had had to keep us on the little she earned as the local excisor, which just about allowed us to exist. So when this mediator arrived from my husband, my mother told him, 'Your friend must first hand over to his wife what it has cost to maintain her and the three children for six months, and then we must agree together on the conditions under which she can return to her own home.' 'He will do that,' the friend declared. Three years have passed and he has still done nothing, either for me or for his children. Meanwhile I have been able to put a little money aside from what I have earned, first by selling fried cakes, then *pagnes** which I dyed with indigo. I paid for dressmaking classes with my savings. Now I am a dressmaker, as the sale of *pagnes* is not very remunerative nowadays. So, I am able to pay my own way, look after my children and help out my mother.

---

* *Pagnes* are lengths of woven cloth; tied around the waist, they can be worn as undergarments or can be knotted over a camisole as everyday wear. (Translator's note)

At the moment, three married men who all believe in polygamy are courting me, but I'm not interested in them. I'm not prepared to accept any man who asks me, although my family and acquaintances try to persuade me it's time I got married again. I'm waiting till I find a good man I can trust.

A year after I left Abidjan I heard that the woman my husband claimed he had married – although this was not true – had left him for a man who was better off than him. That was about the time I received his last letter telling me that I was the only person he loved, that he had been deceived by the other woman, that he was ruined, that he needed me, that he loved me more than ever. The words of the repentant sinner!

At the end of that year I got the religious divorce I had asked for.

Médina

I had the good or bad fortune to be born into a very traditionalist family, very attached to ancestral values and customs. So I was married off to a so-called cousin, who was studying in Saudi Arabia and whom I'd never seen before. When I was at the end of my second year in high school, I was told that my grandfather, a marabout wielding absolute power in the family and thought of as 'God-the-father' by a great number of people including my parents, wished to see me. He had so much authority that his children, nephews, disciples, and all those surrounding him, never argued with his decisions. When I arrived at his house, accompanied by my parents, he said, after the formal exchange of greetings and polite formulas,

You have always been a good and obedient child. I know that you are also a good pupil. I would like to give you in marriage next Friday (this was a Saturday evening) to your cousin X, who is continuing his studies in Saudi Arabia. You probably don't know him, but he is a good boy, very studious and well-bred. He will be an excellent husband for you. He will be back here for the summer holidays next year.

After the wedding, you will return to Saudi Arabia with him and stay there till he has finished his studies.

I was thunderstruck. How could I argue with someone whose word was law, even to my parents, who had never questioned a single one of his decisions? What arguments could I offer and how? Should I storm and rage at this negation of my whole being? For everything had occurred, in fact, as though I did not exist; everything was decided without my having any say in the matter. I did not have the courage to be the only one to challenge, there and then, a decree coming from our religious leader – my maternal grandfather. I was struck dumb, but I did my best to hide my feelings, as my education and my socio-cultural milieu demand.

'What do you think of this plan?' the old man added, trying to read in my eyes some expression of delight, some happy thoughts. But I kept my eyes very obviously lowered. For in my country, among certain sections of the Fulani people, it is a sign of respect never to look one's elders in the eye. He believed this to be a sign of consent. 'So, my child, you agree, don't you?' he said. 'That is good. She agrees.'

I hadn't said a word. But I was in a torment, torn between my desire to say NO and the wish not to vex my parents, but my silence mortgaged my whole future. To demonstrate their approval, my parents said, 'Father, this is a good thing. We congratulate you on your choice, which delights us. We are very grateful to you.' After that, we left.

The marriage took place as arranged. My husband was not present at the ceremony (he was still in Saudi Arabia). It is quite customary in Black Africa for marriages of young couples to be contracted by the parents, in the absence of one or both of the young people. I did not receive any letter or photograph from my husband, until after I had become his wife. The holidays came to an end and I returned to school. I was a boarder in Saint-Louis, some distance away from my parents' home. That year I was in the sixth form. During that period I fell head over heels in love with a boy named Demba. He was a student at the University of Dakar. He lived with an uncle who worked in Dakar during the week, and was able to give Demba a lift back to Saint-Louis at the weekends, when we were able to meet. I was so madly in love with Demba that I couldn't bear the thought of sharing my life with any man but him. I began to feel increasingly rebellious, and this feeling of rebellion was strengthened by my love for Demba and his for me. By the end of this school year, I knew beyond a shadow of doubt that I could not tolerate this marriage to my cousin any longer — a marriage that was to be consummated as soon as he returned from Saudi Arabia.

When I returned home for the holidays, Demba had no compunction about visiting me. My father, who missed nothing and had, moreover, a keen understanding of human nature, took note of the frequency of these visits. He was not a man to mince his words and one day, when Demba and I were in our sitting room, he asked me to leave the two of them alone. He gave Demba to understand, in no uncertain terms, that I was married and that, consequently, he did not wish to see him so often in his house.

After this point had been made clear, Demba left; this did not prevent our meeting outside my home. Finally, the month arrived when my husband was to return from Saudi Arabia; then the week when the marriage was to be consummated. Previously, as soon as I had come home from school, I had confided in one of my grown-up brothers, telling him that I didn't love this husband who had been foisted on me, and that I wanted none of this marriage. He was very understanding and said, 'In that case, you won't have to go through with it. You can get a divorce and marry the man you love'. I felt reassured, like a patient who comes away from a visit to a doctor reassured by his lies. I felt comforted. I had found an ally in my brother. He went to see my mother and told her of my decision. 'Incredible!' she said, adding, 'She never said a word to us'. First of all, my mother thought it was a bad joke. But she quickly realized how I felt when she called me to discuss the matter. My father was put in the picture. He summoned me there and then, together with my elder brother and my two sisters who were supposed to be backing me in my resolve. He used more or less the same words as my mother had in her discussion with my big brother. 'You were in agreement when your grandfather proposed to give you in marriage to your cousin.

You're not going to start making difficulties now, just before your wedding night. Let me not hear anything more of this tiresome talk.' Turning to my big brother, he went on, 'As for you, Moussa, you mind your own business. I don't want to hear any more complaints from you about anything. And that goes for both of you as well,' he added, addressing my two sisters. As my father exercised great authority over us all, no-one had the courage to add a word, except my big brother, in whom I had confided. But when he tried to explain how I felt about my marriage, father shut him up, threatening to beat him. For some reason I felt impelled to stand up to my father myself, just as this meeting was breaking up. But it was too late. I didn't feel strong enough to face him all alone. I would have to put it off to a more opportune moment. From that moment I refused to eat anything that was put in front of me, beginning a sort of hunger strike. All the same, I managed to go and get at least one meal with a girl friend, who lived quite near us, or else I grabbed a sandwich at one of the little food shops kept by Moors in Dakar. On the third day of my 'hunger strike', I was again summoned by my father. He spoke to me in the presence of my mother. 'What's come over you? You've not eaten anything at home for two days. I'd like to know the reason. Are you ill? What's happening?' 'Nothing's happening,' I replied. 'In that case, I want to see you eating your usual meals in the normal way. And above all, don't forget that your wedding night is in three days' time.'

'In three days, that remains to be seen,' I thought resolutely. The next day I once again refused to eat. At lunch time, when I was sitting in my room, my father burst in and rushed at me with a huge stick. 'Are you trying to make a fool of me?' he shouted. 'I told you you weren't to go on refusing your food. This has been going on for three days. Now we'll see if you're going to eat today or not!' I screamed as the blows rained down on me. My mother and brothers rushed to my room and tried to restrain my father, who was lashing out at me with a violence unusual for him. To work himself up into such a state he must have felt that his self-esteem was under attack, that his pride as a father was threatened. His sacred authority was being challenged. That's what he couldn't accept. Any more than I could accept the intrusion into my life of this husband I had never set eyes on.

'Now, I'll kill her,' my father was shouting, in his fury. Nevertheless, I managed to escape from the room, screaming that I didn't want this husband, while my mother and brothers tried to pacify my father. I rushed out of the house, but not wanting to provoke a scandal I stayed on the opposite pavement.

A few moments later, my brothers came to look for me. They said they were sorry for me and begged me to come home. I wouldn't listen to them. My mother then sent our maid to fetch one of her best friends who was like a second mother to me and in whom I could confide. She finally persuaded me to go home, after first getting the assurance that my father wouldn't beat me again. The situation hadn't really improved as far as I was concerned. My parents were prepared to agree to anything I wanted, except what really counted for me: the divorce. They always ended up by countering any objections with their favourite argument:

> She's not the first girl to have no say in her own marriage, and she won't be the last. And, in any case, she did agree when her grandfather suggested it to her. Her cousin K married a man she'd never seen before, didn't she? And look how happy she is with the fine little son she's had.

'Oh!' I thought, 'in that case, if the fact of having a child is a sign of conjugal bliss, it shouldn't be difficult to achieve, unless one is sterile.'

Next, my mother's friend took me aside into another room, so that we could talk calmly of the problem that had brought me into conflict with my parents. Then she returned to consult them. Finally, she came back to me and said, 'Your father is fully determined to kill you and then to commit suicide if you refuse to obey your grandfather's decision. You must understand him. He has always been most obedient to his own parents, as well as to your maternal grandfather, who is also his uncle. You may remember that the same day that your marriage took place, he also gave one of your cousins in marriage to one of your grown-up brothers, who is thousands of miles away still. Your brother will soon be 30, while your cousin is only 14. But you mustn't feel so despairing. If you really consider me your friend, even as a "little mother", you won't refuse me the one thing I am asking you to do: to apologize to your father and say you accept the marriage.' My heart was very heavy. Even my best friend was in collusion with my parents. Deep inside, I felt a great sense of loneliness. I loved my father. He was an upright, loyal, decent man who had always tried to instil into my brothers and myself the idea of absolute obedience to parents and elders. But I loved myself too ... I don't know how I finally gave in to the urgent pressure of my mother's friend.

Alas! The fateful day of my wedding arrived. My grandfather had ordered sheep to be sent to my parents for the festivities, to provide food for all the guests. From morning to evening all the members of our extended family, including the most distant relatives, arrived from all parts. As soon as night fell, the dinner was served. My husband's friends were present, but I had not invited a single one of my own friends, as I had no heart in the celebrations. However, most of my female cousins were there. I sat beside my husband, surrounded by a few relatives and friends of my husband's who delighted in making jokes. At about half past eleven, some of the guests began to leave. Then my mother's friend, the one who was a sort of godmother to me, came to fetch me and gave me certain recommendations before leading me off to the bridal chamber. Early the next morning, some of my aunts came back to the house. Everyone was delighted to find out that I was a virgin. They weren't particularly worried about what I might have suffered. I say 'suffered', for when a virgin sleeps with a man she does not know and does not love, it is tantamount to rape. With death in my heart, I let myself be taken by this man. I can still see the white *pagne* that I wore for my wedding night. The same white *pagne*, now stained with blood, that my aunts proudly exhibited the next morning as proof of my virginity. When I think of all that, I say to myself that I'd have done better to lose my virginity to Demba, which would have put my aunts in an awkward dilemma. Perhaps they would have had recourse to the trick of sprinkling the bride's *pagne* with chicken's blood.

This bit of cinema saves the 'honour' of the family in cases where the young bride has taken certain liberties before her marriage.

According to the tradition in certain circles the festivities lasted a week, during which presents were exchanged between my husband's family and mine. After my wedding night, I refused to have intercourse with my husband. Not being able to persuade my parents to arrange a divorce, I hoped that my uncompromising attitude towards my husband would quickly cause him to consider this solution. And so it turned out: dissatisfied with his new wife, he terminated the marriage a few days after the festivities.

Thus, finally, what I had hardly dared to hope for, happened. With this outcome, I was the first to challenge indirectly any decision of my grandfather who arranged marriages for his sons and his nephews, his daughters and his nieces, as well as his grandchildren, as the fancy took him. The only thing I found revolutionary about him was in the matter of dowries: he asked for only modest sums from the future husbands. In so doing, my grandfather never failed to point out to the suitor, 'I am not selling goods. It is my daughter (or niece or granddaughter) that I am giving in marriage.' If the young man's family insisted on my grandfather accepting more money for the dowry, he would reply, 'Keep the money. It will be useful to the young couple. You'll have plenty of opportunities for spending it.'

Nevertheless, in addition to this modest sum, which in any case is only symbolic, many abuses were perpetrated, unbeknown to my grandfather, by some people who expended colossal sums for the wedding celebration. Only those who obeyed him blindly refused to go against his orders.

When all's said and done, my grandfather had many good qualities. He had a highly developed sense of humanity, as he saw it. Human virtues were more important to him than material goods. But his general outlook on life did not correspond to mine.

Tabara

I am 33. I was married for the first time when I was 16, to a man I had not chosen, a forest warden. I was taken out of high school to marry him. After two years of marriage to this man, who was ten years older than me, my existence was hell on earth. At the slightest disagreement between us, he beat me. In the end, we got divorced. But I had a child by him during the first year of our marriage.

Three years after this catastrophic marriage, that is to say when I was 19, I fell in love with a married man. He divorced his first wife to marry me. With him I believed that perfect happiness was possible. We had three children. I did not work outside my own home. I looked after the house and the children. My husband earned enough to keep us. I was happy in my situation as a housewife, although from time to time my financial dependence embarrassed me. I sometimes found myself refusing to indulge in things that I would have liked to have or do. My husband was nine years older than me. He was a civil servant.

Our love affair went smoothly until he began to go out quite late in the evening, or at unaccustomed times during the weekend. It seemed to me that he found far too many excuses for having to go out. When I couldn't put up with his erratic behaviour any longer, I had a showdown with him. The next week he was more reasonable. He avoided his many unusual outings. 'You must strike while the iron's hot,' I thought. But I soon had to sing a different tune. The following week he resumed his bad habits. I was going out of my mind with jealousy and fear of staying all alone in our house which was isolated on the outskirts of Dakar, with no company other than sleeping children. So that I should not feel so isolated, I sent for one of my younger sisters and a young cousin. I tried in vain to be patient. Two months passed. My husband took more and more liberties. Our relations did not improve. Things went fom bad to worse between us. In desperation, I then decided to go back to my parents. I informed my husband of this decision. Once again he played for time. I was then six months pregnant. He went out, perhaps without my knowledge, but he was not overdoing it.

Three months later I gave birth to my fourth child – the third with this husband. After the birth, I asked my husband's permission to go to spend a month with my parents (to recuperate and get back my strength). In fact, young women often go back to their parents for a rest after having a baby. It seemed quite natural to me that I should do the same. On my return from this holiday, I was treated as if I was simply the watch-dog. My relationship with my husband got worse by the day. I very soon realized that he had taken a mistress. I didn't know what to do. I loved my husband and didn't want to divorce him. I was determined to struggle on. But the more I gave in, the more unbearable he became to me. The more I resigned myself to being patient, the more determined he seemed to try me, as if he deliberately wished to provoke me. I felt completely abandoned. When I was at the end of my tether, I once more got a divorce. I must point out that, apart from my husband's attitude and behaviour towards me, my relations with my sisters-in-law did nothing to help the situation. They really hated me. They didn't miss a single opportunity of making trouble between me and my husband, who was extremely attached to his whole family.

Once more, I found myself divorced and back with my parents, not with one child now but four. Fortunately, my parents could manage to keep me and my children. My two ex-husbands didn't give me any alimony. I could manage quite well without. However, at this period I wanted a job, so as to be financially independent. I got the idea of learning to type. The only qualification I had was the school certificate. If I hadn't been forced to leave school to get married, I would by then have finished university. But, alas . . . After studying for two years I obtained my typing diploma which allowed me to look for a job.

As I'm the sort of woman who won't consider the idea of extra-marital sex, I married again, only to discover that my husband was impotent. I married him three years after getting my typing diploma. Before that, I had lived five years with my second husband. Now I had the terrible experience of finding out about my husband's condition. (Was this accidental impotence, the Xala* brought on by a curse, or congenital impotence? I never knew.) I had to wait six months before I could get a separation from this man, who seemed to suffer from congenital impotence

---

* Impotence that is brought on, it is said, by the curse of a marabout.

(I never had any proof that it had been brought on by anyone). So those were the three men that I had known in the space of 12 years. After this third divorce, I was disillusioned, dejected. I wanted to be left to myself. But that was impossible. I felt the need to have a house for myself and my four children. But in certain African countries, people look askance at a woman who has had several divorces and lives alone with her four children when she could be with her parents. She'd give the impression of being a whore. So I had to give up the idea, or rather, I tried to give up the need to have a home of my own by agreeing to stay on with my parents. Two years later, under pressure from my family, I agreed to a marriage of convenience. The man in question claimed to be divorced. It never occurred to me to look into his matrimonial situation. What is more, he didn't live in the same region as me, although he came from the same ethnic group. To my very great regret, I found out after our marriage that he was polygamous and that he had not really divorced his two previous wives. In fact, he had abandoned each one in turn after landing both of them with several children. One evening, when my husband and I were in the bedroom, I heard the bell ring. My husband went to open the door. A few moments later a young woman burst into the room and hurled herself at me like a wild beast. Before I realized what was happening, she had scratched my face and called me all sorts of names. My husband, who was in the room throughout this scene, didn't raise a finger. At the time I didn't understand why. The intruder had the better of me. Nevertheless I collected my wits and managed to struggle out of bed. And just at that moment she picked up from the bedside table a huge marble ashtray that my husband had brought back from Italy and hurled it at my head. Instinctively, I raised my arm to protect my face. The ashtray hit my forearm and fractured it. Then I lost consciousness. When I came round I was in a hospital bed. Not only had I got a broken arm, but I found I was miscarrying. I was two and a half months pregnant. All this took place under the worst possible circumstances. When I came out of hospital I was very depressed. I didn't try to make sense out of anything. One thing was quite clear to me, I wouldn't have anything more to do with a man like that, who was not only dishonest but a coward as well. Yet another divorce! I didn't bring a charge against the poor woman. I didn't think it was necessary. I was sorry for her, rather.

And now, I'm 33. For the moment, I've no inclination to remarry. But that doesn't mean that I won't. Meanwhile, I'm broadening my mind. I read a lot in my leisure moments. I'm surrounded by brothers and sisters who've had the opportunity of going to university and I often get into discussions with them. However, I don't regret all these different experiences. They've opened my eyes to marriage and the relationship between men and women in our society. I realize that a society like ours sets no store by women. Men get married when they like. They get divorced when it suits them. For my part, I'll never consent again to the kind of married life I've experienced. I hope that women who have suffered as many disappointments as I have, or who have been let down in the same way, will be more prudent and circumspect in future and won't let themselves be taken in again.

Collective interview recorded in Guinea

The seven men listed below agreed to take part in the interview. All participated in the discussion:

Goureïssi, a civil executive with a university education, aged about 35

Aliou, employed in the navy, with a university education, aged about 30

Thierno, a student, aged about 28

Mamadou, a civil executive, aged over 40

Baba, a workman

Souleymane, an executive with a university education

Lamine, a workman

There were eight women present, including the author. Of the seven listed below, only two actually spoke:

Khadidiatou, a housewife with a secondary education, aged about 25

Coumba, a divorced woman with a secondary education.

A young married woman, attending university

Two secondary school girls
A married woman with primary education
A married woman with no schooling

Gourëïssi: It's my impression that the Guinean woman of today is beginning to emancipate herself. As far as I'm concerned, as an African male perhaps I'll be called reactionary. I'm all for the principle of having several wives, because our Guinean women have got into the habit of not doing much work nowadays. I think that, as far as productivity and production are concerned, if I have three or four wives, at the end of the year I'll find myself with three or four more fields. I think that women can be emancipated. That's quite normal. But the Guinean male ought still to have the possibility of having several wives. Why? Simply because the number of women is greater than that of men. Isn't that so?

[Sceptical laughter from the women]

Aliou: I don't agree with your point of view about the need for a Guinean to have several wives. For a peasant who cultivates his land, to have three or four wives comes down to using them as cheap labour. And that's quite general practice. Here in Guinea, in the villages, it's always the women who work for the men. I can quote the example of one of my paternal uncles, who lived in Boffa. He had four wives; they all worked for him. Because he was the son of a chief, he considered that he didn't have to work. His wives worked for him, cultivating his fields. He spent the whole day sitting in an armchair. He received visitors, organized discussions when he would talk about any old thing. In fact, he was a lazy do-nothing, who, quite simply, exploited his wives. It was understandable at that time, as society hadn't reached the stage of development we're at now. People weren't shocked by certain facts and certain practices. People thought, 'That's quite natural'. This was partly a result of the colonial situation, and partly of customs that were deeply entrenched in people's minds. People were brought up with the belief that women were objects for men. With our society tending to become more modernized, different efforts have been made, directed as much to women as to men. When a women's conference was held, a motion was passed calling for the official suppression of polygamy. As far as equality of the sexes is concerned, a campaign has been launched for the total emancipation of women. Here in Guinea, we think that our struggle concerns the whole African continent. We're trying to set a certain example, to show a way that could be an inspiration to the other African states, leading to the emancipation of women. In fact, as long as women aren't emancipated, a percentage of the population doesn't participate in either economic action or social activities. To a certain extent, the non-emancipation of women is a brake on the harmonious development of the country. New situations call for new structures. And, as far as this measure is concerned, it's inconceivable that one category of society – men – should find themselves in opposition to another category – women – and that the latter should be the victims of the ill-treatment and vices of the former. It's accepted that the campaign for the emancipation of women has begun, but things don't always work out in practice as they are supposed to, because you have to take our upbringing and social origins into consideration: we're formed in a certain way. We are, in fact, the product of our upbringing and the environment in which we are born and grow up, and there are certain things we accept more easily than others, there are concepts which *a priori* seem to be different from what we'd like. Since independence, the State of Guinea has been trying to educate the masses: men as well as women, but the latter especially, because the problem of emancipation is a problem for the whole society, but in the first place it's the women's problem. They are the ones who are primarily concerned. Nothing can be done for them if we don't feel that they are participating to some extent, if they don't show some enthusiasm to follow the direction we'd like them to take.

Awa Thiam: The original question was: what do you think of women, and particularly of Guinean women? You should tell us, as far as possible, not what women ought to do or what they ought to be, but what you really think about their present situation.

Aliou: But to understand women, we must after all talk a bit about their past, their present and their future.

A.T.: That may be so, but you were also talking about women's participation, as if this was something hypothetical, or for the future.

Aliou: Yes, because for the moment there's no total participation. Nowadays, women are beginning to be integrated to a very great extent in different sectors of existence. If their participation isn't yet total, it's not for lack of good will. There is a certain wish to improve women's emancipation, but because things don't generally happen spontaneously in society, we must have a little patience.

Goureïssi: I think we must speak much more concretely here, leaving problems of theory and principle on one side. But we must also see the solutions that we're working towards at the present time. I'd have liked us to tackle the most urgent problems concerning the emancipation of women.

A.T.: Yes, let's say, concrete problems . . .

Goureïssi: Principles are principles. There are plenty of works in which we can find everything we need to know about Guinea's political line on women's emancipation. But in a discussion like this, we're talking about our own lives, our own experiences, our own observations, what we reproach women with, as well as what we'd like to see, first of all at the family level, then at the level of society in general.

A.T.: Yes. I think that the family is the cell that is most representative of the state. In fact, isn't it in some way a sort of miniature state? So, we ought to look at both aspects of the question: the family on one level, as such, and then as a cell representing the state.

Thierno: As far as I'm concerned, you can't talk about African women in general. I'll talk specifically about Guinean women, as they're the ones I know. And if you're talking about them, you must distinguish two periods: before independence and since independence. Before independence, women were used like tools: they were the slaves of slaves.

They were considered as a productive force, working for the benefit of men.

A.T.: I think that's still the case now, as Goureïssi said he'd have liked to have several wives, at the present time.

Thierno: That's the old mentality. The face of Guinea, before independence was as Goureïssi described it. So a man who had no profession or training could marry three, four or ten wives. For example, my paternal uncle had more than ten wives. What did he do? He was the chief of a canton. He would sit from morning to night dictating laws and giving orders. He did nothing as far as production of material goods was concerned. His wives and slaves did all the work (in those days, they still had slaves). So women were relegated to the lowest rank of society. Besides, the old Guinean society was very hard on women. Virginity was demanded of a girl, but there was no control to speak of as far as boys were concerned. There are many constraints put on Guinean women that males are spared: for example excision and infibulation. We had to wait till independence and the first Congress of Guinean Women in 1970 for certain contradictions to be dispelled. It was this Congress that decided to fight for the abolition of polygamy.

Aliou: Correction! The fight against polygamy didn't begin in 1970, but much earlier.

Thierno: Yes, but the Congress passed a motion to this effect.

Aliou: A campaign for this purpose was launched soon after independence. In plays, speeches, meetings, the emancipation of women and the fight against polygamy were the problems most frequently dealt with. We had to wait a certain time before this struggle found concrete expression in rights and duties.

Thierno: I quite agree. The struggle didn't begin in 1970. But we know that since independence there has been a gradual effort to get women more involved in production.

A.T.: Didn't women make any effort to involve themselves?

Goureïssi: Yes. They did try. They took part in all the main struggles in this country.

Thierno: Women have been a very lively force, even in the struggle for power.

A.T.: Wouldn't the women be able to tell us about this?

[Silence from the women, who were probably intimidated by the presence of men.]

Thierno: They *can* tell you about it, but since they haven't made up their minds to do so, we men are giving you our opinion. It's true that we had to wait till independence for this emancipation of women to make its mark and express itself. One of the results has been for women to become technicians. If women have been heard on Radio Guinea, it's only since independence.

Aliou: To be exact, Guinean women on Radio Guinea.

Thierno: To give you an example of how little good will men had towards women, when the law against polygamy was promulgated, there was a lot of opposition in certain quarters. It was thought that the Party which was combating these customs was in conflict with the interests of the people. There were uprisings; people thought they would have to divorce their old wives and only keep one. That was how certain people interpreted it.

Goureïssi: Women are trying to keep pace with men in the field of the economy.

Thierno: Here in Guinea, we have women in the police force, just as we've got women governors, women deputies and women ministers.*

A.T.: But shouldn't the women be speaking for themselves? The reason why we were keen to organize this collective interview was so that there could be women present as well as men.

[Silence from the women.]

Aliou: So now you understand why our sisters have been 'inferior' to us up till now.

[Laughter]

Mamadou: Here's your proof. They all keep quiet when they ought to be speaking out.

---

* Only one minister. [Author's note]

A.T.: This morning I was told that women have an inferiority complex in relation to men. I didn't believe it, but now . . .

Mamadou: If men always have to speak for women, of their future, of what they ought to be, that means that up till now they've not understood anything.

Goureïssi: So I must be right to want to have fifteen wives?

[Laughter from the women and the men.]

Mamadou: I'm going to ask you women a question. What sort of relationship would you like to have with your husband?

Khadidiatou: As I didn't prepare anything . . .

Goureïssi: But nobody prepared anything!

Khadidiatou: I didn't expect questions like that. In any case, as far as my relationship to my husband is concerned, I'd like it to be correct.

Mamadou: For example, suppose there are problems, decisions to be taken.

Khadidiatou: In such cases, I'd like my husband to consult me, and for us to discuss the problems together.

Aliou: Leaving him a share of the responsibility?

Khadidiatou: Yes.

Goureïssi: Some men say, 'When my wife and I agree about a problem she's the one who makes the decision. When we don't agree, I'm the one to decide.' Isn't that true? It usually happens like that with married couples. Insofar as I'd like to have a modern marriage, my wife and I put our heads together, we discuss matters. But often the wife doesn't make a decision. When a problem is put to her, she says, 'I don't know; do as you like'.

A.T.: The husband often makes decisions without consulting his wife.

Goureïssi: That does occur, but it's mainly due to the fact that the wife won't agree to share the responsibility for the decision. That's often the case.

Thierno: But there's also the masculine pride of the Black man that's at stake.

Goureïssi: Yes, that's another aspect of the problem to be considered.

Mamadou: I must remind you that when I asked about the

relationship between husbands and wives, it was to give the women a chance to say how they'd like their lives to be with their husbands, how they'd like their children to be brought up . . . what they reproach their husbands with.

Baba: Suppose Madame K. was my wife. Would she agree to my being away from home from early morning till four in the afternoon and then, as soon as I got in, I'm out again till one o'clock in the morning, without telling her where I'm going?

[Lively reaction.]

Khadidiatou: What woman's going to put up with that?

Thierno: These are futile questions. They're quite superfluous.

Aliou: They might seem to be futile questions, but they really go quite deep.

Thierno: Let's consider women in different spheres of social activity.

A.T.: We're talking about the family situation, and the relationship of husbands and wives.

Aliou: Yes, that's the fundamental issue. When a woman isn't used to exercising responsibility in her own home, it's difficult for her to do so outside the home.

Thierno: Who must help her in this respect, if it isn't her husband?

A.T.: The problem is not of helping the women. We're trying to get to the real issues.

Baba: And supposing I was chasing after another woman, what would be the normal reaction of my wife?

[Silence from the women.]

Thierno: When Baba intends to take another wife, he finds it quite fair. But as soon as he discovers that his wife is making a cuckold of him, he demands a divorce on the spot. And when he wants to take a second wife, he insists on the first one giving in to his whims and accepting the presence of the second woman. So the position of men is a contributory factor, among others, to slowing down the emancipation of women.

Thierno: A man should put himself in a woman's position, getting down to her level, to understand her better.

Mamadou: Inasmuch as women are men's equals, we can't accept your expression, as you contradict yourself. When you say that a man must put himself at a woman's level, that means that she's his inferior.

Thierno: No. I'm not saying he must lower himself to her level, but put himself on the same level, or rather, put himself in her place.

Aliou: Inasmuch as a woman is a man's equal before the law . . .

Thierno: . . . in rights and duties.

Aliou: Yes, in rights and duties, I can't imagine that when a man wants to take a second wife, his first wife would ever agree to it.

A.T.: That's the very reason why we'd like to give Baba a chance of explaining to us why he'd like to take a second wife, when he's got one already.

Mamadou: That's a question for all the men to answer.

Baba: Here in Guinea, when a monogamous or a polygamous man has domestic problems, he tends to take a second (or third) wife.

A.T.: Instead of trying to solve his problems with each one?

Baba: He doesn't get a divorce, he keeps his first wives and marries again.

Mamadou: Eventually, the first wife rebels, and rightly so. Either she gets a divorce, or else she appeals to the law, otherwise she has to resign herself. The co-wives usually do the same.

Souleymane: Yes, but now, for a man to be able to remarry, it depends on his first wife.

Goureïssi: It's not always because a man has problems with his wife that he wants to marry another woman. It may be purely and simply out of weakness, a desire for change all the time.

A.T.: For change?

Thierno: It may be a taste for novelty.

A.T.: Isn't that just making excuses for polygamy? Men claim all the rights, women have none.

[The women signal their agreement. The men smile.]

Thierno: It's not an excuse, it's inconstancy.

Aliou: It's irresponsibility.

Thierno: Why should a man claim the right to have ten or more wives when he doesn't give a single one of them the right to have a lover, or even less to have two husbands at once?

Aliou: It's pure selfishness. It's contempt for women. But, if this does happen, it's because the wife isn't really responsible. If she was responsible, it wouldn't occur to the man to take another one, because he knows that he's got someone at his side who won't let herself be trodden on.

The young divorcée, aged 35: Don't you believe it!

Lamine: Aliou is very naive!

[Silence.]

Khadidiatou: Goureïssi, why did you speak of three or four wives, just now?

Goureïssi: No, I spoke of having 15 or more.

A.T.: But could you tell us how many you've got at the present time?

Goureïssi: Me? I've got one. (*A half smile*]. But the question should have been, how many I'd really like to have. To tell the truth, with my present one, if it had been possible to have half a wife, I'd only have taken half a wife. But in Guinean society as it is at present, I'd need fifteen wives. As I've noticed that Guinean women don't do much work. They've become very lazy. They've become 'emancipated'. Emancipation, for a lot of them, means lazing around, dressing up smartly, getting out of the house, going for walks, not having to look after the children. Really, they neglect their duties in favour of less important things. And, as a man, in Guinean society, you can still make demands of a woman.

A.T.: Why make demands, if there is equality?

Goureïssi: No, wait, let me explain. I said that in Guinean society at the present say, I'd need 15 wives. Because this equality between men and women isn't yet effective. So, if I've two wives, and things are not going right with one of them, I'll neglect her for the second one, so forcing the first one to behave as I want her to. And if I've got three, it's even easier. And if I've got 15, I can make them all work. And this way, I can keep them all in line.

A.T.: But that's exploitation and oppression.

Goureïssi: But I force them to work.

Mamadou: Forcing them to work is a good thing, but I don't think it's the right way.

A.T.: They can work of their own free will, without being part of a polygamous system.

Mamadou: I don't agree with Goureïssi because he gives himself rights that he shouldn't have and that the law doesn't give him. He places himself outside the equality of rights and duties of men and women.

Khadidiatou: I don't agree with Goureïssi either.

[Muffled protests from the women, but none of them speaks out.]

Mouna

(A housewife, aged 43, married to a Muslim religious leader. She has ten children.)

I got married when I was 16. I've had 12 children by my husband, of whom two died in infancy. I am my husband's first wife. I've had 13 co-wives, of all different ages, but nine of them got divorced. The youngest is 20, while my husband is over 50. We didn't all live in the same compound, not even in the same town. At present, there are four of us, and we all live in the same house as that is what our husband wishes. Our husband has to travel a lot. We see very little of him. As the first wife, I've witnessed everything that goes on in our home. When the new wife arrives, she's coddled and made much of. She's the object of a thousand and one attentions on the part of our husband. A little while later, she's dethroned in favour of a new co-wife, or because our husband has to undertake another trip somewhere. As far as this is concerned, married life seems intolerable. As long as we wish to please, as long as we're docile, unobtrusive, faithful, there are no problems with our husband, or rather he's got nothing to reproach us with. It doesn't matter whether we're dissatisfied with the life we lead with him. It's two years since I had 'relations' with my husband. My co-wives and I have all been abandoned in favour of the new bride who is six years younger than my eldest son and four years younger than my eldest daughter.

Although I've been deserted as a wife, I haven't been able to do as some of my co-wives have done, that is to say, get a divorce or take a lover; my only thoughts have always been for the future of my children. What would become of them if I was separated from their father? The eldest is 26 and the youngest is only three. My eldest son and his two younger sisters are married. They plead with me not to get a divorce and to look after their little brothers. But must I make the best of a bad job? Just look at the situation my co-wives are in.

The younger co-wives are in the habit of taking one or two lovers every time our husband goes on a long trip. So it has often happened that they were expecting a baby by their lover before our husband got back from his travels. This has occurred three times; in each case there was a divorce. Recently, one of my co-wives who has felt neglected since the arrival in our home of our husband's latest wife, has had no compunction about giving in to one of our husband's disciples who was making advances to her. He has visited her quite openly. Now, people are saying that her last-born is not our husband's child but that of her lover. Either our husband doesn't know what has been going on, or else he's had enough of this sort of incident: anyway he has baptized this child as his own. And the lovers go on seeing each other as before.

As far as I'm concerned, I've never known any man except my husband. I had a traditional, strict upbringing. Although the idea of getting a divorce has passed through my mind, it would never so much as occur to me to deceive my husband. But that doesn't mean to say I condemn my co-wives, for all that. I don't condemn the three who were divorced on grounds of adultery, nor the other six who asked for a divorce because they couldn't stand this polygamous existence. I can understand them all perfectly. They are young. They need to be loved and to feel themselves to be alive. One must recognize that a triangular household – a husband with two wives – cannot be compared to a normal married couple, so even less is a polygamous household with umpteen wives. Dissatisfaction, neglect, desertion are often the reasons for the reaction that throws a woman into the arms of another man.

Awa Thiam: Don't you think you are being hard on yourself and indulgent to your co-wives? At 43 a woman is still young.

Mouna: Oh! I'm already a grandmother.

A.T.: That doesn't matter. You're still young. One last word: do you think that the wife of a religious leader has an easy time?

Mouna: Easy? I don't know. But I can assure you that over and above the respect shown to a religious leader, his wives are also respected by his disciples. Some of them go so far as to venerate the wife who enjoys their leader's favours; that may be from fanaticism or out of self-interest. My life has been rich in experience. It has taught me to understand women and to understand myself a little. If I had to relive my life over again, even at my age and with all the children I've had, there'd be no problem. That's because I've seen so much ... I've had to put up with so much.

A.T.: What can one do in a situation like yours?

Mouna: If you don't get divorced, there's nothing you can do except bear with it all. The Muslim religion is strict on this issue.

A.T.: So, according to you, there's no other solution except divorce or devotion?

Mouna: As a Muslim, I can see no other.

A young woman

(An unmarried mother, aged 18 with no schooling. She is the daughter of a Muslim religious leader in Mali.)

I come from a Muslim family. My father is a religious leader. None of my brothers or sisters have been to the French school. We've only had a Koranic education. Decisions are always taken by my father, even in things that concern his grown-up children. So, in this way, two of my elder brothers and two of my sisters were married without being consulted. Not a single one of them felt the need to protest. My father is as revered by his disciples as he is feared by his wives and children.

A year ago, I was expecting a child by a man my father wouldn't let me marry. Today, I should be carrying this child in my arms, but unfortunately it died . . .

At this point, the young woman burst into tears and could not continue her story. We learned eventually, from her close associates, that she had buried her child herself immediately after its birth, with the collusion of her mother and a third person. Her father was polygamous, so her mother had several co-wives: three to be exact, and nine children. She thought that her daughter's pregnancy not only exposed the girl to scandal but the mother too, and if her husband heard of the affair he might repudiate her and drive her out of the house with her daughter. In countries where the influence of Islam is very strong, an unmarried girl who falls pregnant is considered to be a loose woman. It's the same for all unmarried mothers. It was out of the question for the father to be informed of his daughter's condition, any more than of the birth of the child. Hence, a dissimulated pregnancy. Then – an infanticide.

The body, hastily buried in the courtyard of the house, was discovered a few days later, revealing this odious crime. The girl's father was never informed. Who was at fault? Society? Were you not at fault? Was I? Was it not due to the uncompromising attitude of a man who sows terror in the hearts of his wives and children? Was not this terror the cause of the infanticide? And over and beyond this terror, is it not patriarchy at work, speaking its name? What purpose does this terrorism serve? To dehumanize, to kill.

It is men's cowardice (men who impregnate women to whom they are not married, whom they do not intend to marry, or even to live with as man and wife, who do not intend to recognize their children or contribute to their maintenance), added to their terror of the girl's father or brother, that is often the cause of infanticides or of children being abandoned. So, it sometimes happens in Black Africa – although such cases are rare – that an infant is abandoned near a church or in a dustbin. It is not lack of maternal affection that makes a woman abandon her child. It must be with anguish in her heart that she parts from this little creature that has lived inside her for nine months: her baby. Black, White, Yellow, is any woman to be condemned who abandons her child? If she had wanted this infant to be born, if she had been in a position to look after its material needs, provide for its upbringing, and supposing that she had been able to brave a patriarchal system, would she not have acted quite differently?

Coumba

(A Senegalese woman of the Fulani ethnic group, aged 22, working in the manufacturing industry.)

I'm married to a polygamist who works in the same factory as me. That's how we got to know each other. We got married six years ago and we've two children. We were a monogamous household until last year, when my husband brought home another woman – his second wife. Up till then, we'd never had any problem making ends meet. But, for some time now, we're constantly getting our water and electricity cut off. The wages of the two of us aren't enough any more to meet the expenses of a polygamous household. My co-wife, who's just a 17-year old, doesn't work. At the moment she's pregnant and financially dependent on our husband. She's full of fads and fancies and involves him in all sorts of extravagant expenses. Before the 20th of every month we're practically penniless and forced to ask for an advance on our wages or get into debt. We're behind with our rent. And, after all we must see that there's food for the children. It's not at all pleasant to live like this. And it's not easy either.

> *Awa Thiam:* Do you see any possibility of this situation changing or any solution to your problems?
> *Coumba:* I think that everything will go from bad to worse, or else everything will be all right.

A.T.: That means?

Coumba: Either we'll continue to be buried in debts and get turned out of the house. Or else my husband will find the means of meeting the needs of a polygamous household. I wasn't consulted when my husband took a second wife. I wasn't informed of his intention to get married again till the last moment. Let him find a way out of things now that he's created the problems. Otherwise he'll either have to divorce the second wife or I'll divorce him. I'm not going to go on working for her to sit around all day getting fat with nothing else to worry about except dressing herself up and waiting for our husband to come home every evening.

A young woman

(Aged 38, married to a bigamist.)

I lost both my father and my mother before I was 11. I was married at 15. I live with my husband and co-wife in this village where my eight children were born. My husband took a second wife 12 years ago. My co-wife and I get on very well. Our relationship is quite good. Besides, I was very keen for my husband to take another wife, as I was worn out with my large number of children and having to look after the house and to work in the fields. My husband is a peasant, but I do most of the agricultural work. As I felt that I needed some help, I had no hesitation in suggesting to my husband that he marry again. The second wife now helps me. Let's say that since she's been here we share the work: the housework and the work in the fields. So far, I don't regret that I suggested my husband taking another wife. Today, I've got an ally in her: she is a help to me in every respect. We realized that we have common interests. Usually, during the rainy season, unless there's some physical obstacle like an advanced pregnancy or illness, we spend most of our time cultivating our husband's fields. However, we've noticed something: after the rainy season, our husband goes to sell the crops in the town, while we stay in the village. When he comes back, he takes the trouble to bring food and sometimes he buys clothes for us and the children, but he scarcely ever gives us any money, except what we need for daily food shopping. We need things that we can't have. My co-wife and I have done without things for a long time and now that our crops are doing better, we'd like not to do without things so much, but alas!

Nowadays, what vexes us a great deal and what we complain of a lot about our husband is that he spends a lot of money outside the house. He's even thinking of taking a third wife. Neither my co-wife nor I want him to. At the moment he's courting a youngster of 16. My co-wife and I don't need any help, we can manage quite well. We'd rather our husband did something for us, so that we don't always have to do without things that we can afford from our work. But the unfortunate thing is that, as in most African tribes and societies, the husband has the last word in everything. So he can dispose of our own property as well as his own. At the moment I can't take any action against my husband; nor can my co-wife, although we don't approve of his plans. We've let him know this, but it doesn't help.

Ekanem

(A Nigerian teacher, aged 40)

I am an English teacher in high school, like my husband. I was married in a registry office. Our marriage was what is known as a love match. We first got to know each other in high school. Eventually we both went to study in England. We continued going out together. After living together for a year, we got married. Since our return to Nigeria, our way of life has been rather unusual for our society. To tell the truth, we can scarcely be called a conformist couple. In other words, we have challenged many of the traditional customs. You could say that we are fairly liberal. That shocks a lot of people, but it's our deliberate choice.

I made a point of pursuing my studies fairly far to ensure that I'd never be in the position of the housewife-slave. I've always been put off by the picture of these passive, fatalistic women shackled to a prison-household. At the same time, I've always been sorry for them, and that's what possibly motivated me to go as far as I could with my education, to be sure of economic independence. I've got five children. My husband and I share the job of looking after them. According to our respective timetables, one or other of us takes them to school and goes to collect them. The oldest is ten and the youngest is two. My husband has always agreed that we share the household chores when the maid is off duty. He was also quite ready to change the babies' nappies or bath them if I was busy with something else. Here in Nigeria, some people criticized our way of life, saying it was too westernized. Certain people made no bones about implying that I wore the trousers and that I led my husband by the nose. This was so with quite a number of my in-laws. The fact is that in Black Africa people are more used to seeing a man go out to work for his family's daily bread and not to have to see to any domestic chores when he comes home. That's the tradition. If he doesn't abide by that, people like to say his wife's got him under her thumb.

When my husband and I first set up house together, we were determined to withstand all opposition in our commitment to defying convention. But when we put our ideas into practice, we met with a lot of criticism and people made allegations about us that were quite unfounded. There came a time when my husband got fed up with all the unpleasant remarks. He began to find sharing domestic chores objectionable. There was no longer any question of his looking after the children. At first, this didn't bother me as I had a young cousin living with me and she helped in the housework. But I still boil with fury when I recall what certain people delighted in saying when they came to visit me. 'The wife must work her fingers to the bone for her husband if she hopes to go to paradise,' they said, adding, 'it's written in the Koran.' I was often tempted to retort, 'Crap! Mind your own business!' But given the society I'm living in, duty demanded that I show them respect, so I held my tongue.

In the end, my husband lost all interest in helping with the household chores. I restrained myself, with difficulty, until the day I discovered he had a mistress. Then I had no compunction in having it out with him, but in a quite reasonable way. I finally let him know that I wasn't going to be put upon, if he wasn't prepared to play fair with me. His sole reply was that there was nothing between him and this woman who was said to be his mistress. But a few days later I had proof to the contrary.

There and then, out of defiance or spite, I don't really know, I took one of his best friends as a lover. When he found out, he was wild. I was ready to go on with the affair, although I wasn't that keen. But he immediately broke with his mistress, and began behaving decently again. I loved my husband and I knew that he loved me. There was no question of a divorce as far as I was concerned.

Today we are less sensitive to other people's criticisms and less influenced by what people say about the way we run our home, which makes our life together much easier.

A young woman

(A teacher, with a B.A. degree, aged 30)

My life has been quite different to that of an older generation of women. Until I finished high school, I lived with my family and had to conform. When I finished school, I had to be responsible for myself, as I was leaving home for the first time to go and live in a university residence. As far as I was concerned, the end of my schooling marked the beginning of my political initiation. And, coming into contact with boys, I had to form opinions on different problems I'd never previously thought about, like politics and sexuality. I became active in a militant students' organization, and went to live with a fellow student. When my parents heard about this, there was a scandal. I come from a very traditionalist family who can't conceive of a girl having any sexual freedom before she's married. During my period of militant activity, I had cause to change my sexual partners for one reason or another (either our opinions clashed or we went different ways). Finally, after I'd been living for a year with a boy who was also a student, the two of us decided to get married. My parents were by no means in agreement. They would have preferred to choose a 'fine gentleman' themselves for their daughter's husband. It didn't take me long to make my decision. My own future was at stake. I broke with my family. My marriage took place. I was sorry to be obliged to break with my family, but I had no choice. I've had two children. At the moment my parents are making timid efforts to re-establish relations with me. I don't hold anything against them.

Part 2: The Trials and Tribulations of the Black African Woman

The problems that beset Black women are manifold. Whether she is from the West Indies, America or Africa, the plight of the Black woman is very different from that of her White or Yellow sisters, although in the long run the problems faced by all women tend to overlap. Their common condition is one of exploitation and oppression by the same phallocratic system, whether it be Black, White or Yellow. In Africa as in Europe, it is not unusual to find battered wives; in Europe as in Africa there are polygamous husbands. Whether polygamy is institutionalized or illegal, it is imposed on women by external forces. Women are still, in our own day, considered as objects, as sub-human. Everyone behaves as if women had no human sensitivities. The most convincing example of this is when little girls are married or betrothed as soon as they are born. In a country like Mali, and particularly in the Segu region, families can be found in which all the daughters are betrothed very young, some having been promised in marriage at birth. The reason given – true or false – is the wide-spread practice of polygamy, which would soon make for a shortage of wives. But this is only a hypothesis. If this partially explains the custom of child brides, it by no means justifies it. Among certain ethnic groups, the Tukolor and Fulani for instance, it is frequently accepted as a tradition.

Sometimes, these marriages may be contracted for reasons of social prestige. When a man marries a girl of 'good family', he acquires greater social consideration, more respect. So, as soon as a son is born, some men hasten to ask for the hand of a girl for their son, sometimes before she is even conceived.

Polygamy seems to be rampant in every country in Black Africa. In the Republic of Guinea, which claims to be progressive,

and whose first president, Ahmed Sékou Touré, opted for a socialist state, women are faced by the same problem as their Senegalese,
Malian, Ghanaian or Nigerian sisters.

Polygamy continues to exist there, in spite of measures taken,
not to forbid it, but to limit the number of people who practise it.
So we read the words of the then President of Guinea, Sékou
Touré, in Pierre Hanry's *Erotisme Africain* (p.74):

> Guinean women must not be instruments of production in
> the economic life of the nation, nor domestic instruments in
> the life of the family. They must be workers, aware of the
> economic improvement of the nation and equal partners in
> the home.
>
> Young people of Guinea, polygamy is in your hands: you
> can maintain it or see that it disappears, according to the
> quality of your education and your strength of will in build-
> ing a new Africa which will be permanently rid of the infer-
> iority and oppression of women.

Hanry then goes on to say,

> Unfortunately as in all areas where it was exercised in 1965,
> the revolutionary action of the Secretary-General of the PDG
> (Parti Démocratique Guinéen) seems in this matter to have
> scarcely gone beyond the stage of words. (p.75, *op. cit.*)

Polygamy certainly still exists in Guinea at the present time,
but Pierre Hanry's point of view in this matter is not necessarily
the correct one. To present the problem in this way is to blind
ourselves, consciously or not, to the real issues. Arbitrary measures that the masses, especially women – the principal people
concerned – cannot understand, will not help us arrive at equality
of rights and duties, which still have to be defined. It is only by
unremitting struggle that women will succeed in forcing action to
be taken whereby they can obtain little scraps of equality, and in
the end an equality that is imposed on everyone and observed by
everyone.

The countries of Black Africa must certainly overhaul their

economies, but social reform is also necessary. A close look must be taken at customs since, if women are to be liberated, the prerequisite must be a change in people's mental attitudes. In fact, there would have to be a total upheaval in the colonial and neo-colonial structures that still exist in Black Africa, and by this we mean a radical revolution. To conceive of the liberation of Black African women on any other footing is to delude ourselves. We deliberately speak of 'liberation' of women, in preference to the term 'emancipation', as the latter word suggests *a priori* the idea of a typical infantile character of women. It reduces a woman to the status of a minor, a child whom it would be necessary to emancipate. Is this not in fact what a large number of people think? And perhaps this is how we must understand the subjection of women.

We had to wait until the sixteenth century before women were acknowledged to have souls. How much longer must we wait before it is conceded that Black folk, and more especially Black women, also possess this attribute?

On the practical level, irrespective of all religious considerations, what is the situation respecting polygamy nowadays? In any European country, when a husband goes in for that form of semi-condoned polygamy that consists of taking a mistress – or several – the wife can have recourse to the law by instituting action for divorce, or at least obtain support for better treatment from him. Such a course of action is not possible for a Muslim woman, who grows up in a system of institutionalized polygamy, where this is not permitted. What is more, such action would appear aberrant in a Black African context, in which marriage is generally religious, not civil. This difference between the situation of Black and White women is found at practically all levels. And this is the main basis for our claim that the Black woman's struggle is of a different nature from that of her White sister. The majority of European women do not lack essentials, whereas Black women are fighting for survival as much in the field of institutions as in the manner of her daily existence. In other words, European women can gain much more advantage from their struggles – even if these don't lead to a radical revolution and a total upheaval of social structures. Where Black women have to combat colonialism and neo-colonialism, capitalism and the patriarchal system, European women only have to fight against capitalism and patriarchy.

1. Clitoridectomy and Infibulation

In his book, *La Cité magique et magie en Afrique noire*, Jacques Lantier describes an operation as follows:

> The woman in charge of the operation first takes hold of the child's labia majora and labia minora, separates them with her fingers and secures them with large thorns stuck through the flesh on the inner aspect of the thighs. She then takes a kitchen knife and slits the head of the clitoris (the prepuce), before cutting it off. While another woman mops up the blood with a rag, the mother scrapes away the skin the whole length of the clitoris with her finger nail. No-one takes any notice of the child's heart-rending screams. When the mother reaches the root of the clitoris, finally disengaging it, she resects it with the tip of her knife. Her assistant again mops up the blood which spurts out. The mother lifts up the skin, separating it completely from the flesh. Then, with her hand, she makes a deep hole, which bleeds profusely. All the women of the neighbourhood, who have been invited to watch that the operation is correctly performed, dip their finger, each in turn, into the wound, to make sure that the clitoris has been completely removed.

Then the operation continues:

> After a brief moment's respite, the mother picks up her knife again and cuts away the labia minora... Next she abrades the edges of the labia majora with the knife, exposing the raw flesh... When the wound is quite open and raw, she makes several longitudinal incisions, then pricks it all

over with the point of the knife . . . Having thus completed the abrasion in the regulation manner, she brings the labia majora together while they are still oozing blood and joins them with long acacia thorns . . . The mother completes her operation, making sure to leave a very narrow orifice, just sufficient to allow for urination and menstruation. (*op. cit.* pp.277-8)

While we do not challenge Jacques Lantier's description, we do wonder if it is in fact the mother who operates on her own daughter, and if other women have the right to mess around with the excised girl, as he reports. However, his account of the way excision and infibulation are practised, far from giving us essential information about the characteristics of the tribe in question, reinforces our impression of the cruelty associated with these operations, which constitutes for us a basis for their condemnation.

The origins of excision and infibulation

Excision and infibulation are practised nowadays in the Ivory Coast, Burkina Faso (originally Upper Volta), Mali, Guinea, Niger, Senegal, Somalia, Sudan, among the Afar and Issas, in Saudi Arabia, Egypt, Ethiopia, Yemen, Iraq, Jordan, Syria, Southern Algeria and Benin. In the countries of Black Africa, Muslims, Christians and Animists are alike affected. We find the custom among such ethnic groups as the Tukolor, the Diolas, Mandingoes, and some sections of the Serer tribes. It is widespread among Muslims in certain Arab countries. In view of the controversy that rages between the advocates of excision and infibulation and those who want the total abolition of these practices, it is necessary to take a look at their origin.

It is often said that the practice of excision originated with Islam. In fact, there is no allusion to this in the Koran, the basis of the Muslim religion, which can be verified by referring to the Arabic text or to the translations into different foreign languages. So the Muslim religion is certainly not its source. Why then is excision generally associated with Islam? The following is the gist of information obtained from inquiries among the Arab chroniclers and religious leaders of Muslim communities in Black Africa:

Long before the time of Mahomet, there was a prophet named Ibrahima (Abraham), who was married to his cousin Sarata (Sara). He went up to the land of Gerar where reigned King Abimelech who delighted in taking unto himself all men's wives who were remarkable for their beauty. Now it happened that Sarata was unusually fair. And the king did not hesitate to try to take her from her husband. A supernatural power prevented him from taking advantage of her, which so astonished him that he set her free. And he restored her back to her husband and made her the gift of a handmaid named Hadiara (Hagar). Sarata and her husband lived together for a long time but Sarata bore Ibrahima no children. And eventually, Ibrahima took Hadiara to wife: some say that it was Sarata who said to her husband that he should take her handmaid to wife, since she herself could bear him no children. And so Sarata and Hadiara became co-wives to Ibrahima. And Hadiara bore him a son and his name was Ismaïla (Ishmael); and Sarata also bore a son to Ibrahima and he was called Ishaga (Isaac).

In the course of time, the relationship between the two women deteriorated. And so it came to pass that one day Sarata excised Hadiara. Some say that she only pierced her ears, while others maintain she did indeed excise her.

On this point there is disagreement between the different chroniclers. Some say that excision became current practice among Muslims, from that day onwards. Nevertheless, it is tempting to ask why all Muslim women are not excised. In the Bible, there is no mention of excision, any more than in the Koran. The story of Hadiara is told in the Old Testament as follows:

Now Sarai, Abram's wife bore him no children; and she had a handmaid, an Egyptian whose name was Hagar. And Sarai said unto Abram, Behold now, the Lord hath restrained me from bearing; I pray thee, go in unto my maid; it

may be that I may obtain children by her. And Abram heark-
ened to the voice of Sarai. And Sarai, Abram's wife, took
Hagar, her maid, the Egyptian, after Abram had dwelt ten
years in the land of Canaan, and gave her to her husband
Abram to be his wife. And he went in unto Hagar and she
conceived: and when she saw that she had conceived, her
mistress was despised in her eyes. And Sarai said unto
Abram, My wrong be upon thee: I have given my maid into
thy bosom; and when she saw that she had conceived, I was
despised in her eyes: the Lord judge between me and thee.
But Abram said unto Sarai, Behold thy maid is in thy hand;
do to her as it pleaseth thee. And when Sarai dealt harshly
with her, she fled from her face. (*Genesis*, 16, i-vi)

Diverse interpretations have been put upon this ill-treatment,
inflicted on Hagar by Abraham's wife Sara.

At the time of the prophet Mahomet, excision was already a
current practice. He neither forbade it nor advocated it. Hence
the ambiguity of the formula which, as Benoîte Groult reminds us,
constitutes the sole reference to excision found in the Hadiths: 'Do
not intervene in a radical fashion; it is preferable for the woman.'
(*Ainsi soit-elle*, p.106. Everyone interested in excision and infibulation should read this work, the first in which these practices
are analysed from a political viewpoint.)

As for infibulation, its function, which has nothing to do with
any religion, escapes no-one. It constitutes the most eloquent
expression of the control exercised by the phallocratic system
over female sexuality.

Contrary to excision, male circumcision is, in the Islamic as in
the Jewish religion, the sign of a covenant between God and
Abraham and his descendants after him. Thus, we read in the Old
Testament:

And God said unto Abraham, Thou shalt keep my covenant
therefore, thou and thy seed after thee in their generations.
This is my covenant which ye shall keep, between me and
you and thy seed after thee; every man child among you
shall be circumcised. And ye shall circumcise the flesh of

your foreskin and it shall be a token of the covenant betwixt me and you. (*Genesis*, 17, ix-xi)

Some first-hand evidence

P.K.: I had just turned 12 when I was excised. I still retain a very clear memory of the operation and of the ceremony associated with it. In my village, excision was only performed on two days of the week: Mondays and Thursdays. I don't know if this was based on custom. I was to be excised together with all the other girls of my age. Celebrations were held the previous evening. All the young and old people of the village gathered together and stuffed themselves with food. The tomtoms were beating loud, late into the night. Very early the next morning, as my mother was too easily upset to have anything to do with the proceedings, my two favourite aunts took me to the hut where the excisor was waiting with some other younger women. The excisor was an old woman belonging to the blacksmiths' caste. Here, in Mali, it is usually women of this caste who practise ablation of the clitoris and infibulation.

On the threshold of the hut, my aunts exchanged the customary greetings and left me in the hands of the excisor. At that moment, I felt as if the earth was opening up under my feet. Apprehension? Fear of the unknown? I did not know what excision was, but on several occasions I had seen recently excised girls walking. I can tell you it was not a pretty sight. From the back you would have thought they were little bent old ladies, who were trying to walk with a ruler balanced between their ankles, and taking care not to let it fall. My elders had told me that excision was not a painful operation. It doesn't hurt, they repeatedly assured me. But the memory of the expression on the faces of the excised girls I had seen aroused my fears. Were not these older women simply trying to put my mind at rest and allay my anxieties?

Once I was inside the hut, the women began to sing my praises, to which I turned a deaf ear, as I was so overcome with terror. My throat was dry and I was perspiring though it was early morning and not yet hot. 'Lie down there,' the excisor suddenly said to me, pointing to a mat stretched out on the ground. No sooner had I lain down than I felt my thin frail legs tightly grasped by heavy hands and pulled wide apart. I lifted my head. Two women on each side of me pinned me to the ground. My arms were also immobilized. Suddenly I felt some strange substance being spread over my genital organs. I only learned later that it was sand. It was supposed to facilitate the excision, it seems. The sensation I felt was most unpleasant. A hand had grasped a part of my genital organs. My heart seemed to miss a beat. I would have given anything at that moment to be a thousand miles away; then a shooting pain brought me back to reality from my thoughts of flight. I was already being excised: first of all I underwent the ablation of the labia minora and then of the clitoris. The operation seemed to go on for ever, as it had to be performed 'to perfection'. I was in the throes of endless agony, torn apart both physically and psychologically. It was the rule that girls of my age did not weep in this situation. I broke the rule. I reacted immediately with tears and screams of pain. I felt wet. I was bleeding. The blood flowed in torrents. Then they applied a mixture of butter and medicinal herbs which stopped the bleeding. Never had I felt such excruciating pain!

After this, the women let go their grasp, freeing my mutilated body. In the state I was in I had no inclination to get up. But the voice of the excisor forced me to do so. 'It's all over! You can stand up. You see, it wasn't so painful after all!' Two of the women in the hut helped me to my feet. Then they forced me, not only to walk back to join the other girls who had already been excised, but to dance with them. It was really asking too much of us. Nevertheless, all the girls were doing their best to dance. Encircled by young people and old, who had gathered for the occasion, I began to go through the motion of taking a few dance steps, as I was ordered to by the women in charge. I can't tell you what I felt at that moment. There was a burning sensation between my legs. Bathed in tears, I hopped about, rather than danced. I was what is known as a puny child. I felt exhausted, drained. As the supervising women who surrounded us goaded us on in this interminable, monstrous dance, I suddenly felt everything swimming around me. Then I knew nothing more. I had fainted. When I regained consciousness I was lying in a hut with several people around me.

Afterwards, the most terrible moments were when I had to defecate. It was a month before I was completely healed, as I continually had to scratch where the genital wound itched. When I was better, everyone mocked me as I hadn't been brave, they said.

A Malian woman, aged 35 with a university education, who works in a government department. She has been excised and infibulated. Awa Thiam: What is your opinion of excision?

I have to say that excision and infibulation are deeply rooted in our society. Even if girls and young women nowadays protest against these pracices, we must recognize that their protests meet strong resistance on the part of older women, as is proved by what happened in my family.

After my personal experience of all the troubles, physical and psychological, that can result from excision and infibulation, I decided, with the full agreement of my husband, not to have our three daughters done. They were all born in France while my husband and I were finishing our studies. When we returned to Mali, my mother was the first to ask me whether I had had my children excised and infibulated. I replied no, and made it clear that I had no intention of doing so.

It was during the long holidays. As I had found a job, I often left my children with my parents and went to collect them at the weekends. One day, on my way home from work, I dropped in at my parents' to see my children and to say hello. I was surprised that there was no sign of my daughters. Normally they ran to greet me. I asked my mother where they were. 'They're in this room', she replied, pointing to where they were accustomed to sleep. I wondered if they were sleeping, or didn't know I was there.

I went into their room. They were lying on mats on the ground, covered with a few *pagnes*. At the sight of their swollen faces and eyes full of tears, I gasped and a cry escaped me. 'What's the matter? What's happened, children?' But before the children or the two women who were with them could reply, I heard my mother saying, 'Just see you don't disturb *my* grandchildren. They were excised and infibulated this morning.'

I can't tell you what my feelings were at that precise moment. What could I do or say against my mother? I felt a surge of rebellion but I was powerless in the face of my mother. My first reaction was to burst into tears. One of the women present said, 'You should be pleased that everything went off all right for your daughters'. The other one said, 'She's just overcome with emotion!'

Rather than risk showing a lack of respect to older women, which is strongly disapproved of in my circle, by telling them what I thought of them and the way they had acted, I hurried away from the house. In view of the state they were in, there was no question of my taking my daughters home. They had to stay there till they were healed. Like many African women, my mother had just proved that she had rights not only over me, but also over my children – *her* grandchildren. In fact it is common in Mali for children who are sent to spend their holidays with their grandparents, to come home circumcised, excised and/or infibulated.

A.T.: Do you think it is possible to put an end to these practices?

I can't say for absolutely certain, but I don't think it's impossible. At what cost? I don't know. But nothing can be done to abolish them unless the women concerned group together to impose their point of view.

Mata, a 29-year-old married woman with a B.A. degree. She has been excised and infibulated.

I have no memory of being excised or infibulated as the operation was performed when I was very young. I only became aware of my condition when I was 20 and about to get married. I had grown up in a society where sex and sexuality were taboo subjects.

As soon as I was conscious of being excised and infibulated, I felt a deep sense of outrage. What was I to do, I wondered. I had no intention of letting myself be cut open with a knife on my wedding day, as is the custom for all women who have been both excised and infibulated. Then it occurred to me that I could be operated on at the hospital. I first applied to doctors and then to midwives, only to meet with a refusal each time. At one time I thought that a social consensus was at work. Every single person I spoke to was against the operation. Both men and women who I'd asked to operate on me at the hospital looked at me as though I was a rare animal. One doctor had no hesitation in saying, 'You want me to make it easy for you to gad about?' He almost threw me out of his consulting room.

Day by day, I grew angrier and more rebellious. I saw how strong social pressure could be. My wedding day grew nearer. My chances of avoiding the 'kitchen knife operation' grew slimmer. Finally, on the evening of the wedding I had to make the best of a bad job and let myself be cut open.

Is Mata the only woman who has tried to rebel? How many women from Mali, Senegal and elsewhere, who have been both excised and infibulated, have seen their solitary, inarticulate attempts at rebellion come to nothing?

Madame X, aged 44, a Senegalese woman belonging to the Tukolor ethnic group. Aïssata, aged 12, a Senegalese girl of Mandingo origin.

Aïssata was put in my charge when she was three. When she turned six, we sent her to school, contrary to the wishes of her parents, who live in a village. She continued at school till she was 12. Before she could take the end of year exams, including the primary school certificate, she was faced with a problem that involved us all – my husband and our own children. Her father had come to take her home, with the intention of having her excised and infibulated. Naturally, he knew that I had not had my own daughters done, nor his, and that I did not intend to do so. When Aïssata got to know the object of her father's visit, she ran away: She disappeared from the house for three days. On the fourth day I found her wandering near the house and I brought her home.

During her absence, her father had been making the most unpleasant scenes. Every day he planted himself in front of our house, shouting at the top of his voice. It seemed as if he was deliberately trying to provoke a scandal. He loudly denounced us for having had his daughter educated. 'I've lost my daughter,' he kept yelling. People came running from all over the neighbourhood, to our great embarrassment.

As soon as Aïssata was back with us, her father lost no time in forcing her to go back to the village with him. As there was no train that day, he took the bus. We were powerless to stop him. What right had we to oppose Aïssata's departure? None at all.

A few days later we learned that Aïssata had been excised and infibulated, to our great distress.

A young woman from Mali, aged 26, divorced with one child. She has a degree in economics.

Awa Thiam: What do you feel about the problems of excision? Do you consider it to be a mutilation or not?

'I was excised as a child. I'm talking about my own personal experience. Today, I'm glad I had the excision operation. The reason why I maintain this point of view is that it has fulfilled its function as far as I'm concerned. I've been divorced for four years and I've never for one moment felt the desire to run after a man, or felt the absence of sexual relations to be a lack, a vital lack. That indicates to some extent the function of excision: it allows a woman to be in control of her own body. And that's why I don't in any way consider it as a mutilation.'

A.T.: Nevertheless, it's surprising that, with all the information you have about the practice of excision, you should consider your excised state as a source of satisfaction. A woman can very well exercise control over her own body without being excised. As far as that's concerned, excision is not a necessity.

'I don't agree.'

A.T.: But look! If I understand you right, clitoridectomy must be perpetuated, since it renders a service to women. Have you ever stopped to think what this operation represents? What is the function of the clitoris? It seems to me that every human organ has a very definite function to perform. And to remove one is tantamount to a kind of mutilation, and that's all the more true as it concerns the clitoris. So, wherever you have clitoridectomy, there is mutilation.

'Yes, in that sense there is mutilation. But I can't think of excision, as practised by our elders, who haven't been taught about these things, as being a mutilation; in fact it all boils down to what the intention is – and with them it isn't to mutilate. So, on these grounds, I don't think of myself as having been mutilated. Nevertheless, if I let my own child undergo this operation, I would consider it as a mutilation, because, even if I have no personal experience of the role of the clitoris, I have learned from books, from medical information, all about the troubles that can result from excision.'

A.T.: Do you think that our elders don't know why they make their children undergo clitoridectomy? One is tempted to believe that they are fully aware of what they are doing. Didn't you say that you felt – or rather that you could consider yourself lucky that you had had this operation, as it allowed you to control yourself and feel no sexual desire? Doesn't it occur to you that this is just what this practice is for? Nowadays there are plenty of women who are well aware of the troubles that result from this operation, but they still continue to have it performed on their children and grandchildren.

'I find it hard to explain . . . but I still don't think of clitoridectomy as a mutilation.'

[Silence]

A.T.: Have you any sensation in the place where the excision was made?

'Yes.'

A.T.: What are these sensations like? Painful or pleasant?

'Pleasant, on the whole.'

A.T.: And infibulation? What do you think about that?

'I wasn't infibulated. But I imagine that the sole aim of this practice is to prevent a girl from having any "relations" before she is married. Quite apart from the atrocity of the actual operation, I think it should be condemned on the grounds of the dreadful effect it continues to have on the woman's body.'

What results from this interview is the manifest desire to absolve our elders, on the grounds of their ignorance of scientific information about clitoridectomy. This is to underestimate them. According to the women we have questioned, the motive most frequently evoked was the influence on the sexual life of girls. What emerged as we talked to different women was the following idea, expressed in one form or another: a woman must be made solely into an instrument of reproduction. Any enjoyment on her part constitutes a potential danger to the man, or at least he is led to believe this. But the paradox is that polygamous men prefer non-excised women. So who benefits then from clitoridectomy? Neither the woman nor the man. Yet it enables the latter to have as many docile, submissive women under his thumb as he wants.

We are not talking here of sexual pleasure, but one may well wonder what is the point of reducing the sexual life of a woman to her reproductive function, while naturally it consists of more than that. Why hack away women's genital organs, when they themselves do not explicitly demand this practice? Does this not constitute alienation? And should not these practices be banished henceforth from every society, on the same grounds as any mutilation perpetrated on the mind or body of any human being?

Are excision and infibulation sexual mutilations?

Such a question may seem *a priori* superfluous, ridiculous even, to some people. But because of the divergence of opinion about these practices, it is a question that we are forced to ask.

Silence has long been observed about excision and infibulation. With the exception of some colonials, who write about them as mutilatory practices, nothing has been written or done about this matter until quite recently. Today, a timid interest is being taken in them. But very few people undertake to talk about them, on the grounds that these are traditional customs and rites.

But how are they viewed by the people who practise them? We shall analyse a few cases, those of Mali, Somalia and the Afars and Issas.

In Mali, we must make a distinction between two ethnic groups who practise excision: the Bambara and the Dogon.

With the Dogon, excision is obligatory. According to Dogon cosmogony, it is necessary because a girl contains some 'male' element in her as well as the female, and reciprocally for the boy. So it is essential that the element which is contrary to the true nature of each be eradicated, so girls must undergo clitoridectomy and boys must be circumcized.

With the Dogon, excision and circumcision serve as a purification ceremony. They also mark a sort of coming of age for the young Dogon, so they are seen as a means of emancipation for adolescents. This, then, is a rite of passage into a group or class in which one is taken seriously and considered as a responsible person. 'The child can undertake nothing serious as long as he is not circumcized,' states Marcel Griaule in his work *Dieu d'eau* (p.149). In other words, a boy ceases to be a child as soon as he is circumcized. Similarly, a girl cannot be considered to have reached full 'womanhood' until she has undergone excision. Since excision is thought of as the purification of the feminine element, it implies the idea of perfectibility in the adult. In this ethnic group, circumcision and excision are certainly not seen as sexual mutilations, although medically and physically they may be viewed as such, not only by foreigners, but by those on whom they are practised. However much a little girl may want to be excised because all the other girls of her own age have been done, or because she has been persuaded that it is the right thing to have done, this does not mean that she doesn't suffer excruciating pain. Similarly, she feels that violence is being done to her body; she is conscious of suffering a physical injury, of being maimed in some way. Whatever other people may claim, what she experiences is a mutilation, even if she has heard it repeated time and time again that her clitoris is a masculine element which has no place in her body and so must be removed. If excision had not resulted in disastrous consequences in the sexual life of Dogon women, we might have been able to shut our eyes to the matter. But it is the cause of frigidity and sometimes – even if rarely – of death.

In spite of the reasons evoked by the Dogon to justify excision, it still remains at the present day, a mutilatory practice.

With the Bambara, excision and infibulation are traditions which are centuries old. In the course of our research, we consulted Islamic religious leaders and Muslim zealots, the majority of whom could give us no better explanation than that they practised excision because they followed the Muslim religion. To our rejoinder that there is no mention of this practice in the Koran, we always received the same reply, the gist of which is that Mahomet said to Um Atiya, an excisor, 'Do not operate in a radical manner ... it is preferable for the woman.' (We find this same recommendation quoted by Ahmad Abd Ar Raziq in *La femme au temps des Mamelouks en Egypte*, p.205.) They add that he did not say 'no longer operate', nor did he say, 'do not practise excision'. From these replies it would appear that for some people – the passionate upholders of excision – it was condoned by the prophet Mahomet, inasmuch as he did not prohibit it. On the other hand, the opponents of excision submit, rightly, that Mahomet in the matter of excision is ambiguous; this explains why certain Muslim societies practise it while others do not. As for infibulation, no explanation, based on religion or myth was given to justify it. Its primary function is to prevent girls from 'taking certain liberties' before they are married. In an article on the women of Somalia, which Annie de Villeneuve published in the *Journal de la Société des Africanistes* in 1937, 'Étude sur une coutume somalie: les femmes cousues', she submits that infibulation in this country is 'an absolute guarantee that the girl has not been touched, a guarantee that the parents give on her value as merchandise'. In the case of the Bambara, it is not a question of the parents wanting to benefit from the girl's virginity, or any speculation on her marriage value; it is more a matter of honour, which reveals their attachment to ancestral customs. In Islamic societies in Black Africa, it is not uncommon for women to have recourse to trickery to cover up the fact that their daughter had lost her virginity prior to marriage. For example they may display a sheet stained with the blood of a fowl, the morning after the wedding, to give the impression that she has been duly deflowered by her husband. If a girl who gets married for the first time is not a virgin, the honour of the whole family is at stake. Nowadays, Malians tend to be more lax in their observance of customs, but the practices of excision and infibulation persist, except perhaps in certain intellectual circles. Nearly all Malian women have been excised. Only those of the Sonraï tribe are spared; this also goes for infibulation, which, as it happens, is less widespread in Mali than excision.

Apart from loss of virginity, which involves the honour of the whole family, infibulation also rules out *a priori* any risk of conceiving an illegitimate child. Such an event would represent a scandal, something shameful for people of so-called 'good family'. We are tempted to ask our Malian sisters whether they have ever wondered what would happen if their excised and infibulated girls were overpowered and raped. They would then be forced to admit that infibulation is a precarious means of safeguarding a girl's virginity until her marriage. (Note that rape is not such a common phenomenon in Black African countries as in Europe, or rather that it exists in another form: a good number of married women suffer legalized rape at the hands of their husbands.)

We have learnt that it used to be the custom in Mali that when men were forced by drought to emigrate to new lands to try their fortune, they would have their wives partly sewn up. In other words, a second infibulation was performed on these women and they were not opened up again until their husbands returned. That was supposed to 'protect' them from any temptation to be unfaithful, or against any male aggression during their husbands' absence. (Here the function of infibulation is quite unambiguous.) On his return from an absence that might have lasted up to five years, or even longer, the husband would have his wife cut open again with a kitchen knife, by the local excisor; for here, contrary to what happens in Somalia, it is not the husband who cuts his wife open, in order to have sexual intercourse with her. This habit of having a wife 'sewn up' for the second or umpteenth time, when the husband has to go away for long periods, dates back very far. Nowadays, it would appear to be more or less obsolete – or so we are led to believe. In the course of our researches, we were only told about it by very old women, who had neither performed it on others nor had it done to themselves, but had merely heard about it. Whether or not this practice is still current in certain regions or isolated villages of Mali remains an unanswered question, for want of adequate investigation.

To sum up, excision and infibulation, performed by means of resin and acacia thorns, are integral parts of Bambara customs and traditions. These practices have only been questioned quite recently by the National Organization of the Women of Mali. It is important to note that a small minority of women in Mali – both among the Bambara and other ethnic groups, whether intellectuals or not – are at the present time beginning to favour the total abolition of excision and infibulation, which they view as mutilations. This minority will one day make their voices heard; but they will need a great deal of determination.

In Somalia, nearly all women have been excised before puberty. However, it is noteworthy that excision is, without exception, followed by infibulation. To this Somali women owe the designation, 'sewn-up women'. It might be supposed, from this, that they are literally sewn up with needle and thread. In fact, the operation consists of making preliminary gashes in the labia majora and then suturing them together with acacia thorns, the labia minora having been removed at the time of the excision. Resin may also be used. It is as difficult to determine the origin of excision and infibulation among the Somalis as it is elsewhere. According to the religious leaders of this exclusively Islamic country, the only explanation is a religious one. As for infibulation, nobody makes any secret of the reason for this, and its purpose. Its sole function is to prevent girls from having sexual intercourse before marriage, in the name of the moral code which is in force in Somalia as well as in the majority of Muslim states. The other motives, mentioned in Annie de Villeneuve's article, quoted above, smack of colonialism and racism.

We must conclude that, as far as this country is concerned, excision and infibulation are certainly not considered as mutilatory practices. On the contrary, they are insisted on, even today, by all Somali women, from the eldest to the youngest, partly in response to what they see as the relaxation of traditional morals. We discussed this with a married Somali woman, aged 33, with a degree in law, living in France with two little girls who were already attending school. We were shaken to learn that she was determined to have her children excised and infibulated as soon as she returned to Somalia. It was most distressing that the only justification she could put forward to counter our arguments against these practices, was the apparent permissiveness of society everywhere. Her French middle-class education did not lead her to an awareness of the realities of her existence. Let us not forget that French shcools are part of a patriarchal society, transmitting, whether we like it or not, a patriarchal ideology.

Women can and must take up their stance against the condition which is imposed on them. It may seem easier to back down in the face of all their problems, but in reality this will not pay dividends. If they do not challenge the patriarchal society, if they leave everything to be decided by men, they will continue to fulfil the roles that have always been attributed to them: both as ornamental figures and as maids-of-all-work.

Some of our conservative Black African sisters seem to be locked into their situation. So we certainly can't count on them to change the status of Black women. This change will only come about with future generations. Meanwhile, those of the present generations have something to say about their sufferings.

After this brief glance back at the history of excision, we must analyse the importance of these practices as found in different African societies: excision may have a different meaning for, say, the Fulani of Fouta in Senegal to that found among the Dogon or Bambara of Mali, or the Kikuyu in Kenya, and so on.

It appears that for Muslims, excision is by no means mandatory; it is practised by some and not by others. It is a *sunna*. After the death of Mahomet, the *Tabih'un*, or disciples, tried to reproduce all the prophet's actions and exploits as a perfect model for their followers. Thus, they themselves performed everything that he recommended to the faithful. In this respect, we have the following definition of a *sunna*, given by Abdelwahab Boudhiba in his book *La Sexualité en Islam*:

> The historical model, in the person of the Prophet, and described by the Sunna, is an ancient one. We must understand from this that, as time goes on, the further away Muslims become from the facts of history, the more their collective image becomes necessarily falsified ... Far from being the basis for progress, history is reactionary, and as the original models fade into the distance, the more they are exalted, mythified, surrounded by haloes. History, prophecies, legend become indistinguishable.

We are not much wiser for this 'definition', but it explains to some extent the perpetuation of certain actions, such as circumcision and excision, and practices such as polygamy.

Benoîte Groult, in her book, *Ainsi soit-elle* (mentioned above) mentions a myth common to both the Bambara and the Nandi in respect of excision. In the chapter entitled 'La Haine du C...' we read:

> The Bambara excise the clitoris on the pretext that its dagger [sic] can wound the man and even cause his death ... The Nandi, for their part, have observed that girls in whom this harmful organ has not been removed, waste away and die at puberty.

These myths persist to the present day, but the most widespread among the Bambara is that a non-excised girl resembles a boy. In other words, we find the recurrent image of a prominent clitoris which would prevent coitus – because, they tell themselves, it is hard to imagine two boys having sexual intercourse. It's not a question here of homosexuality, as the picture is clearly that of a boy and a girl. But this is the basis for their insistence on the girl being excised.

We must not tackle the thorny problem of trying to reconcile the excision of Hadiara (Hagar) with this explanation of excision. Whatever the explanation, the fact is that men had embarked on

a phallocratic policy of imposing sexual mutilation on women.
Does this then allow us to accept Abdelwahab Boudhiba's definition of the model, quoted above, as correct?

It is difficult to know whether excision is based on one or more
myths, or whether it perpetuates a historic event. Muslim religious
leaders claim that it is modelled on the excision of Hadiara, just
as the faithful on a pilgrimage to Mecca reproduce some of the
actions of Mahomet, and orthodox Catholics try to use the behaviour of Jesus as a model. Would such a practice have come
about spontaneously, or has there been some male intervention
to enforce it? If we discount the religious considerations, it seems
reasonable to deduce that excision was instituted by men to prevent women enjoying any clitoral pleasure and to suppress any
sexual desire in them. The excuse often made in countries where
women are excised is that they are too sensual. The aim of excision would thus be to reduce, if not to eliminate this 'excessive'
amorous desire. But what is the real situation?

The excised woman frequently finds herself reduced to the state
of a vagina and a reproductive machine. Just as in certain societies
men are required to police themselves, through self-criticism, so in
Black Africa it would seem that males have forced women to
become their own torturers, to butcher each other. Women have
rationalized excision and infibulation, associating these with pre-
scriptive practices until they became an integral part of their traditional or ritual body of customs. This would partly explain the fact
that women themselves take the responsibility for their own mutilation. How have excised women come to despise non-excised
women? In the case of the Bambara, we have clear evidence of the
pressure — albeit verbal — that men have exercised over women, to
reinforce attitudes towards these practices and so perpetuate them:
we refer to the justification of excision on the basis of the alleged
'impossible coitus' between a boy and a non-excised girl, which
moreover has nothing to do with the supposed origin of the custom
(i.e. with Sarata and Hadiara) that led to its assuming a religious
character. Men have everything to gain from excision: as Benoîte
Groult states, 'Their wives' sexual desires would thus [by excision]
be greatly diminished, which would be, so they imagine, a guarantee that they would remain faithful.' (*op. cit.*)

Infibulation in addition to excision forces us to deduce that, in countries where these practices are current, men quite simply wish to guarantee the total possession of their wives' bodies. It was never stated in the Koran that infibulation should be practised. The same is true of excision, although Mahomet does mention it in the Hadiths, without, however insisting on the practice. But this is not the case with infibulation. So we must try to find out what is the origin of this mutilation.

We may reasonably postulate that, in their desire to maintain womankind under their total control, men have sought systematically to deprive her of anything which, by virtue of her sex, would procure her any pleasure, especially any pleasure with which they (men) would not be associated. Benoîte Groult gives a good analysis of this in respect of European societies. It is in this light that we must look for the meaning of the 'toothed vagina' found in certain myths, folk tales and legends.

This is illustrated by a Kordofan tale from Leo Frobenius's *Märchen aus Kordofan*, quoted by Pierre Samuel in his study, *Amazones, guerrières et gaillardes*:

A man has an extremely sensual wife who sleeps with all the men in the town. He is most grieved, while knowing full well that if she were faithful to him, she would wear him out. He asks counsel of a friend who advises him to go and settle in another town with his wife. He does this, and when they are settled, he tells his wife that the men of this town have a second penis, and what is more, this is made of steel. The wife is very frightened. Then he tells all the men in the town that the new arrival has scissors with which she cuts off the penis of any man who sleeps with her. In spite of the danger, one of the men courts her and, to defend himself against the scissors, he wears a belt under his clothes, to which he attaches a knife. Despite her fear, the woman begins to caress him under his clothes, and in so doing touches the knife which she thinks is the second penis, made of steel. As she starts away, her rings tinkle against the knife and the man thinks it is the scissors. Both of them flee in terror.

The myth of the toothed vagina is found in many countries: for example, among the Bena-Lulua people of the Congo, in Gran Chaco among the Toba, and among the Aino of Japan. It is surprising to note that the Bambara concept of the clitoris as a dagger is almost identical to that of the Toba, who view it as a residual tooth, presumably all that remains of the toothed vagina. (See Pierre Samuel, *op. cit.*)

Any woman with a modicum of sensitivity must be profoundly shaken by reading about these bloody operations. Benoîte Groult speaks for everyone when she writes:

> These descriptions stab us in the very c[unt], don't they? The pain is felt in our own female organs. We feel sick for ourselves. Our human dignity is hurt. We share the pain of all these women who resemble us and who are denied, damaged, destroyed in that part of themselves which is their very essence. And we feel sick, too, for all those fools who think it essential to be superior in everything and who, to achieve this, have chosen the easiest solution for both man and woman and the one which most degrades them both: to belittle the other. (*Ainsi soit-elle*, p.101)

But there is a choice. We can rebel and fight. And this is what we have done. It would be a fine thing to see all excised and infibulated women rising up in their own countries in revolt against these practices; this would soon sow confusion in the ranks of our Black African brothers. It is a first and very important step to see that the general public is informed, that feelings are stirred up over the fate of the victims and that everyone is made acutely aware of the condition of women everywhere. But this must be followed by practical action. Simply to feel compassion is not enough.

The land of the Afars and Issas

The Islamic community of the Afars and Issas, comprising about 60 per cent of the total population of this territory, strictly enforce the practice of excision, which, as in Somalia, is always accompanied by infibulation. The reasons given are the same as in Somalia. The evidence collected, as much from men as from women, reveals that the majority, if not the totality of Muslim women are frigid and that they have had complications in childbirth. Excision and infibulation are considered as mutilations by most young women. None of them are ever free, for the rest of their lives, from the sense of laceration that accompanies sexual intercourse and their confinements. We see that all women, whatever their origins, present more or less the same symptoms as a consequence of these operations.

The deaths that result from excision and infibulation account for approximately five to six per cent of the annual mortality rate for women. The particularly high death rate here among parturient women is partly due to the low standards of hygiene found in many villages, but also to the persistence of clitoridectomy and infibulation. The principal cause of death is a severe haemorrhage, causing the woman to bleed to death, when the scar tissue that had formed after the operations bursts open. We find similar cases in all countries which practise excision and infibulation. So don't let anyone tell us that these are never a cause of death!

However refined the method used, these operations still involve 'butchery'. In Bamako, the capital of Mali, some excisions are performed nowadays at the Gabriel-Touré Hospital, the only place, to the best of our knowledge, where the patient is anaesthetized before the operation, using a local anaesthetic on the genitals. 'You see there *is* some progress,' Malians who advocate excision would say. Is this not, however, a method of ensuring that clitoridectomy is perpetuated? It must also be pointed out that there are still plenty of women who take their daughters to the local excisor, in spite of the decision taken by the State of Mali to allow these operations to be performed in the hospital. The women concerned are the most traditionalist and conservative. To the best of our knowledge, infibulation is not yet practised in any hospital. But how long will it be before this operation is also performed at hospital level, in the name of 'progress' and 'hygiene'? Meanwhile, the traditional excisors retain a sort of monopoly of this practice.

Bringing the mutilation of any human being whatsoever to public attention is a positive move. Annie de Villeneuve does attempt to do just this in her article on excision and infibulation among Somalian women; but perhaps she could have done this without feeling the need to judge this Somalian society and its rites according to Western criteria. She didn't even take the trouble to get to know the women who have been excised and infibulated, as the following passages testify. Speaking of the women of Somalia she says, 'It is not that they are foolish, but that they are not yet civilized, they are incapable of reason, so that their heads do not tell them that it is wrong to perpetuate this instinct for cruelty which underlies their actions.' (*op. cit.*, p.32)

What is 'reason'? What does it mean to be 'civilized', or quite simply what do we mean by civilization? Crimes have been perpetrated by colonials in the name of 'civilization' (the only one recognized being *western* civilization). They continue to be committed by neo-colonials and by the fascist apartheid régime in South Africa.

Annie de Villeneuve's attitude is not surprising, inasmuch as she is locked into a colonialist outlook. Others have written in the same vein on diverse matters relating to Black Africa. In reply to her and to all the others, we quote these words from Aimé Césaire's *Discourse on Colonialism* (p.9): 'A civilization that proves incapable of solving the problems it creates is a decadent civilization.'

It seems unlikely that de Villeneuve's attack on Somalian society is simply inspired by her disapproval of excision and infibulation. Judge for yourselves: 'In this abominably *venal* race [our emphasis], such a barbaric custom could well have originated from a taste for money and be perpetuated for the same reason.'

What makes this race venal? Is it more venal than any other race? Is it more venal than the race which preys on other races, slaughtering, plundering, deporting? Can one possibly compare the indigenous population of Somalia to that of capitalist France? Surely not.

It should be pointed out that de Villeneuve draws her conclusions from false premises. We must assume that she has understood nothing of Somalian society, or that she has some motive for writing '. . . the girl has no dowry and is quite simply offered for sale. She is nothing more than human capital, exchanged for cattle or cash.' (*op. cit.*)

What is the position as regards French customs, and in particular dowries? This is what Benoîte Groult has to say on the subject: '...a girl also needed a dowry, without which, no matter how great her personal qualities, she would be left on the shelf, with no hope of assuming the dignity that went with marriage.' (*op. cit.* p.126). De Villeneuve interprets this as meaning 'In France, it is the father who purchases a husband for his daughter, as she is incapable of finding one for herself.' Nothing could be further from the truth!

This type of tit for tat argument gets us no further than any similar attempt to define our African societies by comparing them with those of Europe. But people who understand nothing of ritual practices must beware of attacking them, especially when they base their judgement on criteria which bear no relationship to the mentalities of people in the society under consideration.

The women of Black Africa have suffered enough from these colonial and neo-colonial attitudes. Let us have no more of them! This applies particularly to ethnologists, anthropologists, colonialists and neo-colonialists.

For or against sexual mutilation?

There is no need to waste time speculating about the harm that results from sexual mutilation practised on women. There is enough evidence to be found in the French language *Journal of the Medical Society of Black Africa* (*Bulletin de la Société Médicale de l'Afrique Noire*, 1975, vol. xx, no. 3). For example (p.251):

A woman of 23, visited in July 1973, after an altercation between husband and wife. They have been married for 48 hours and the woman is found to have no vaginal opening. She is about to be repudiated by her husband. Previous history: excision at the age of five, before which she presented no genital malformation. Dysmenorrhoea since puberty.

On examination: coalescence of labia majora, with two small openings, an upper one for passage of urine and a lower one through which menstrual blood is passed with difficulty. Vagina opened under general anaesthetic.

A woman of 24, a virgin, complaining of hypogastric pain. On examination, coalescence of labia minora, following excision at the age of fourteen.

A woman of 50, admitted on 11 January 1975 for acute retention of urine. Previous history: excision of clitoris at the age of ten. Difficulty with micturition [urination] for the last 20 years, namely dysuria and pollakiuria (difficult or painful urination]. Acute urinary retention five years ago, treated with a course of dilation.

It is well known that Voodoo as practised by Haïtians entailed a blood pact which gave them the solidarity needed to overcome their enemies. We must remember that Haïti was one of the first islands of the Caribbean to win independence in the nineteenth century. If clitoridectomy were accepted as a sexual initiation rite (which is not universally the case) operating in a similar fashion under a colonial or neo-colonial régime, we might be able to argue in favour of preserving it as a factor for unity. For some people this may indeed have been their argument in favour of preserving the practice.

In Black Africa blood rites, in the form of blood pacts, helped in the formation of blood fraternities. Blood pacts have also been known among Europeans – Greeks, Slavs and some Germanic tribes. These pacts figured the mingling, then drinking, of blood. This practice consolidated the friendship and solidarity of the participants making them into 'brothers'. In such cases, it was not a matter of merely performing some everyday custom. These were functional rites, indispensable to the struggle. It was as if they gave concrete expression to the determination and conviction of people sworn to give mutual assistance to each other in combating hostile, foreign elements, and resolving to give their lives for their liberation and their freedom.

So, it's a question of solidarity. Militant. Combative.

Liberating. The claim that clitoridectomy is a bond between the women on whom it is performed arises by analogy. This argument does not hold water. Must clitoridectomy be demanded of women? Could they not find some other bond which would unite them? Excision could easily be abolished, completely wiped out in Black African societies, without weakening the cohesion of the tribe or the ethnic group. It is not necessarily a factor for solidarity, as some Africans claim.

Let us now turn our attention to Kenya, after hearing Kenyans say, 'We perpetuate the practice of excision because it enables us to enjoy more intense sexual pleasure,' and, on the other hand, 'It is a necessary condition for receiving a complete religious education.' So, in the name of pleasure and in the name of preservation of their cultural heritage! Such are the Kenyans' main arguments in favour of clitoridectomy. This is a country which has opted for progress, and where clitoridectomy is performed on pretty well the entire female population.

Let us cast our minds back to the Mau-Mau uprising. 'Their leader, Jomo Kenyatta,' as Benoîte Groult reminds us, 'educated at an English [British] university, stated quite unambiguously in his book, *In the Shadow of Mount Kenya*, "No Kikuyu worthy of the name would want to marry a girl who has not been excised, as this operation is a prerequisite for receiving a complete moral and religious education".' (*op. cit*, p.105). Benoîte Groult's reference to an English university is particularly astonishing. Does she wish to imply that such a university 'civilizes', completely changes Black people by diverting them from 'barbaric', 'primitive' customs, specific to their people and their tribe? In other words, that such an education alienates them? Certainly it does! And this situation can be perpetuated if Black people do not become aware of what it means to exist as a Black man or woman. Even if such an awareness cannot eliminate this alienation, at least it can help to reverse the process. The fact that some Black intellectuals insist on maintaining the 'barbaric' practices of their ancestors, including excision, may well prove to stem from a concern to recover their essence, their specificity. 'A funny way to go about it!' might be the retort. But this return to one's roots is only a reaction to the colonialism which sought to destroy everything which identified the African as such: self-defence, we might say. But what determines this particular reaction? Let people react, but don't let them mutilate women!

The justification given for clitoridectomy among the Kikuyu in Kenya is that it is carried out under conditions that diminish the pain after the operation. The girls who are to be excised are made to bathe in a river very early on the morning of their excision. They are obiged to stay in the water for about half an hour, and this is supposed to have an anaesthetizing effect on the sexual organs. Only a partial clitoridectomy is performed, as can be gleaned from Jacques Lantier's description in *La cité magique*.

Even supposing that there is no pain, and that the woman can still experience pleasure, is clitoridectomy thereby vindicated? Are Kikuyu women who have been excised free from complications throughout their lives? Do they enjoy sexual pleasure, in spite of their excision, as it is claimed? Do they give birth easily, with less pain than their non-excised sisters? It is surprising to find Kabongo writing

the songs and dances which accompany it [the excision] contain the essential elements of the laws and customs of the community. More than that, they play many roles, including that of a pre-operative treatment which causes clitoridectomy to lose its terrifying character ...

This gives the impression that the author of this passage was unaware of the complications arising from clitoridectomy. It is not simply a question of fearing the operation itself, but more importantly its harmful consequences. Look, for instance, at the three examples quoted above from the French language *Medical Journal of Black Africa*. But later on, this same author continues, 'more personal reasons stimulate the girl to be excised ... she sees excision first and foremost as the means of gaining recognition as a fully-qualified member of the community'.

Who is this writer speaking for? Certainly not the women who have been excised. Can membership of a community not be expressed in other terms? Mutilation should not perform this function, or at least it should only be suggested symbolically.

Conclusion

The question of excision and infibulation is so complex that it must be treated with the greatest possible sensitivity. Are we dealing with practices that women themselves want?

This does seem to be the case amongst some extremist Muslims in countries like Saudi Arabia, Yemen, Guinea and Senegal, where excision is practised systematically. It also seems to be the case where women insist on preserving certain customs in the name of ancestral values, and block latent resistance among those who categorically condemn these operations.

But no, excision and infibulation are not wanted by the majority of young girls for whom they are a real mutilation, a real torture, no matter how much their elders may try to argue to the contrary. We cannot in all honesty claim that all women who have been excised, or excised *and* infibulated, are nowadays against these practices. The majority of them inflict the same operations on their daughters, even though they are aware of the evils that can ensue (lack of sexual response, complications in childbirth and so on). They do it in spite of the wishes of their daughters. In other words, they do it to avoid dissociating themselves from others; because, in their society or ethnic group, it has to be done. But they are by no means convinced of the validity of these practices. So, what action should be taken? Must we categorically demand the wholesale abolition of both excision and infibulation? Theoretically, we would answer immediately in the affirmative. But the question cannot be settled so quickly and conclusively even in theory, especially if we take note of the following passage in Jacques Lantier's *La Cité magique et magie en Afrique noire*. He claims that a form of excision is performed in some French hospitals on middle-class Frenchwomen who wish to increase their capacity for sexual enjoyment:

> We have seen that Kikuyu girls are excised, a practice which would result in loss of sensation from the clitoris were it not for two peculiar practices . . . The Kikuyu 'matrons' do not completely excise the clitoris, but leave a portion which is introverted and which then, owing to the formation of scar

tissue, adheres to the interior of the vagina. This enables a ritual masturbation to take place when the masculine organ comes in contact with this artificially created sensitive knob, and so increases the woman's capacity for sexual enjoyment while respecting the tribal rule. A fairly similar surgical operation has been performed on wealthy patients in Paris over the last few years. I personally know one eminent surgeon who 'doctors' the vaginas of young women by separating the clitoris and folding it back on to the interior of the vagina. It goes without saying that such a transformation considerably increases the sensation felt by the woman during sexual intercourse. The mind boggles at the erotic skills of the Kikuyu (*op. cit*. p.264)

Without a doubt. The question which now presents itself is whether excision inevitably diminishes sexual response or whether it contributes to pleasure. But we are not attempting to hold a brief for mutilatory practices, whatever their origin. If these practices are seen and experienced by women as sexual mutilation, they should be abolished.

Every woman is, or ought to be, concerned about sexual mutilation practised on the body of another, whoever she may be. But it remains for the excised and infibulated women themselves, being opposed to these practices and aware of their harmful consequences, to say publicly that they want an end to these ancestral customs; and to translate their words into action in their daily lives. In other words, let those women who oppose all forms of mutilation begin to set an example and form the core of a campaign on the issues. Solutions aimed at in this way now seem within reach.

Excision: If this is seen to be a mutilating practice, as we believe, then it must be abolished; it must be opposed, here and now, in the same way as forced sterilization such as is practised in some countries of the Third World and contested by movements like Black Women for Wages for Housework, and Grass Roots, in the USA.

Infibulation: No information indicates that it contributes in any way to a woman's sexual enjoyment. According to the case-histories which we have collected, infibulation appears as a mutilation with serious, even dangerous consequences, as much on the physical as on the psychological level. This practice can no longer be tolerated.

The average man or woman in Black Africa does not give much thought to clitoridectomy and infibulation, any more than to the condition of women generally. Within mass Black African organizations, whether of the right or the left, these matters are avoided, on the grounds that they are not apt to mobilize the interest of the masses. Who decides this? Who decrees it? Men, and the dominating ideology of these organizations which, even when they include some women in their midst, are fundamentally mysogonist. If women wait for men to win liberation for all, this will be postponed until 'the dawn of the Great Revolution'. Women must be responsible for their own fate, take their destiny into their own hands, reflect on their oppression and their problems themselves, and face up to the possible solutions. They don't have to break categorically with men, but rather work together with them for the liberation of both women and men, refusing any kind of imperialism (that is, subjection) that the latter might be tempted to exercise over them.

There is every reason for disseminating information among women, telling them what they can expect from excision and infibulation. Let adult women take care of their own bodies.

How to combat these practices?

Is it 'necessary' to attack religion? No, since there is no religious basis to these practices, in spite of certain people's contentions. Then must we attack the social structures which uphold these practices? By all means. But how? By undertaking campaigns through the press, in the countries concerned *and* abroad. Every possible action in this field deserves consideration. History provides an abundance of material from which to draw lessons. We should cast our minds back to the various attempts made in the past to abolish these practices. For example, those of the Scottish Mission to Kenya in 1929 and that of the Society for the Protection of Children, which held a conference in Geneva in 1931. All met with failure.

It is obvious that the struggle against these practices cannot be successfully waged unless we also challenge the current social structures in these countries. Moreover, it is necessary to spread information among the men and women of these countries and others who do not know of or acknowledge these practices, so that everyone may take a stand against them. But what action can we undertake? Will it be theoretical or practical? Both – through spreading information, and then carrying out its lessons. But any external action must be undertaken in alliance with that of the women most affected, or with the movement which represents them. Any other way not only risks failure through being too cut off, but also jeopardizes the action of the militants themselves.

2. Institutionalized Polygamy

All the justifications which people have tried to give for polygamy have the character of *a postiori* rationalizations without real foundation. (Jean Suret-Canale, *La femme dans la société africaine*)

Numerous 'motives' and 'reasons' are invoked in respect of polygamy. From a social point of view, polygamy is considered a necessity in Black African circles. It may be the expression of a desire to increase the number of children and enlarge the family. As such, it implies that children constitute wealth and the larger the family the better. (But better for whom?) A distinction must be made between polygamy in an urban society and that in a rural area.

The essential difference between these two forms of polygamy may appear insignificant to some people. We find that in an urban community only members of prosperous classes (the petty bourgeoisie) can afford the luxury of three or four wives or more. It is true that working-class people also have one or two wives, and so it seems that polygamy among city dwellers is often a means of displaying one's worldly goods. These men want to prove their competence to themselves and to others. It's a sort of luxury. A man of means can claim all kinds of privileges, including that of choosing several wives. In the name of what? A spirit of prodigality, of exaggerated enjoyment? An excessive, capricious sensuality? Everyone agrees that the practice of polygamy is not confined to Black Africa, and even less to Muslim countries. Whether institutionalized or not, polygamy exists in every country, in Europe and elsewhere. Once again, it is the women who suffer the most from this situation. The man has nothing to lose. What does polygamy represent for a middle-class man?

In theory, it is a sign of wealth, of property. But in fact having several wives proves nothing; look at the cases of men who cannot afford to marry, who misappropriate public funds for this purpose and who end up in prison. Are they trying to mislead people? Or is it just a question of brainwashing? The type of polygamy we are considering is that which is practised and institutionalized in Black Africa. So perhaps it should be interpreted here as a promise of *future* wealth, an investment in wives and children? The explanation of polygamy as a sign of real prosperity does not hold water. When one considers that there is a tiny minority of people who are well-off and a disproportionate number of folk who are poor and exploited, it seems that the explanation is simply that polygamous men are selfish, irresponsible, thoughtless, *brainwashed*.

We may well also ask ourselves why, in urban societies, members of the working class, who are far from well-off, are polygamous. Economically, they have nothing to gain from it. The reasons given in the course of our researches among the male population, reveal that for 80 per cent of the people questioned the problem is one of sexuality and has nothing to do with luxury. Two, three or umpteen wives can be explained by the fact that, once she has had a child, the woman who is ignorant of other forms of birth-control abstains completely from all sexual intercourse. There follows a break in the sexual life of the couple which is only resumed when the child begins to walk or talk. This period varies according to different ethnic groups.

This is a reasonable enough method for ensuring a degree of family planning, so that the woman generally has her children at two-yearly intervals. This custom may to some extent explain polygamy in both urban and rural areas. But it certainly cannot justify it. If a woman can abstain from sexual intercourse, there's no reason why a man can't. On the other hand, we might argue for freedom for all, and say: 'Men, you want to be polygamous. Go ahead then, and leave women in peace.' Women also, if they so desire, have the right to polyandry (the practice of having more than one husband) but that's not what they are looking for at the moment. In fact, we are dealing here with a question of equal rights for women. What men do is said to be natural, but women don't even have the right to *want* to act like the men. At this level, we must aim at a radical change in the structure of the family, and, what is more important, in the structure of society.

It must be pointed out, of course, that other solutions to the problem of family planning do exist in the present day. There are the pill, intrauterine devices, the diaphragm and other forms of contraception, none of which involve either women or men in prolonged sexual abstinence. This can no longer, then, be used to justify polygamy, as in the following case where Madeira-Keïta speaks of the Malinké:

> In the absence of satisfactory infant foods, the child depends on its mother's milk for one and a half to two years. And as long as the child is breast-fed, the mother insists on complete sexual abstinence. The husband naturally finds this period too long. Here we see quite clearly the sexual motive for polygamy (*Aperçu sommaire sur les raisons de la polygamie chez les Malinké*)

Why do working-class men take several wives? Apart from the reasons given above, it is probably because they don't see this as a problem in the short term. In other words, as long as the dowry is not very high, they can afford this 'luxury'. Contrary to bourgeois marriages, which are a source of speculation, here the dowry is very modest; it is all a question of class. Nevertheless, the money involved could help to improve the wellbeing of the family, instead of going towards the acquisition of another wife. Sheer brainwashing, and the ease with which marriage can be undertaken in this social category, partly explain the growing incidence of polygamy among working-class people. Here, the wives are herded together in one dwelling, one household where they quarrel among themselves and instil in their children the mutual hatred which they feel towards each other as co-wives. Isn't this to be seen as one of the most harmful effects of polygamy?

As for polygamous marriages in rural societies, the motive which appears everywhere is that of *labour*. 'The more wives I have, the greater my profit-making capacity.' This raises the question whether man's vocation is simply to accumulate material wealth. We do not think so.

For some people in Africa a large number of children is a sign of wealth. 'A large family is rich and respected,' writes Madeira-Keïta. 'The men in a family make up an army.' (*op. cit*.) Are we in such a permanent state of war that we feel the need to create armies? Wouldn't an argument claiming that Black Africa needs heads which think and hands that work be more convincing? The more of these qualities, the better it will be for Africa, for total liberation from the various yokes under which the continent is suffering and being destroyed. But the practical problem is to know what it is possible to do with a mass of young people in an Africa which day by day is further despoiled, ravaged, pillaged and starved by colonial and neo-colonial forces. This in itself is a reason for expanding the number of Africans who will liberate their homeland from colonial or neo-colonial exploitation, imperialism and underdevelopment.

At present, it is a difficult and delicate matter to decide between the limitation of births and an uncontrolled demography. But nothing justifies polygamy. It is the product of a society in which the phallus rules. How does this arise in the different African milieux?

Amongst the well-off, particularly in the case of Muslim extremists, marriages do not have to involve an exorbitant outlay. On the other hand, as we have already stated, marriage can be an occasion for great financial speculation. The girl is as good as sold to the highest bidder. In such cases, marriage is not a matter of affection, but of money. Surely this is scandalous! We women are not goods, non-persons to be disposed of according to parental will, our passage assisted by a certain amount of palm-greasing.

In this social stratum the dowry can reach astronomical proportions. It may be accompanied by gifts: a car, a television, a sewing-machine and many similar goods. This outlay can be catastrophic for the finances of the bridegroom and his parents — if they are not rich and if they share in the wedding expenses, it can sometimes even lead to financial ruin or to prison. This situation may seem incredible, but it is common in a number of African countries, including Senegal. This explains in part the anger that some men feel about such a dowry system. There is for example in Dakar a religious leader, El Hadj Seydou Nourou Tall, the grandson of El Hadj Omar, who gives his nieces and granddaughters in marriage for a nominal sum only. What is more, he takes the trouble to point out to the future bridegroom, or the latter's parents, that this is a marriage and not a purchase. This attitude may seem unimportant, but in the light of the highly commercialized marriages that take place in bourgeois and petty-bourgeois families, it shows a good deal of sense. As each family tries to outdo the other, colossal dowries may cause them to run into debt, unless both are extremely well-off. Suret-Canale confirms this, as we read in his article, 'La femme dans la société africaine' in *La Vie Africaine*:

> While it is true that historically the dowry was a symbol of union, it is nevertheless perfectly clear that the economic aspect, indeed the sordidly commercial aspect, has now overtaken the original meaning which has progressively been obscured.

This opinion is not universally held. For example, Madeira-Keïta states that,

> Generally speaking, ethnographers exaggerate, or more exactly, misinterpret, the economic motives behind polygamy. They have invented inappropriate expressions such as 'marriage by purchase' or 'the bride price'. They explain the polygamous régime as a real and profitable investment of capital, pointing to the work done by wives and their children. (*op. cit.*)

Notwithstanding Madeira-Keïta, there is a commercialization of marriage. The girl becomes a piece of merchandise, circulating by means of this fetish-object – money. This is particularly the case in the Congo where the bridegroom is often asked, after the marriage, 'How much did you pay for her?' a question which refers, of course, to his wife. A dowry which exploits people, a dowry which ruins people, has nothing human about it. It goes against humanity and its development in our African society.

But alongside the detractors of the dowry system, we find those who enthusiastically uphold it. The larger the dowry, they claim, the less likely the marriage is to end in divorce. 'If a man has spent a very large sum to obtain a bride,' the argument runs, 'he'll think seriously before divorcing'. In response, we assert that if a man is determined to leave his wife he will doubtless do so. A dowry, large or small, cannot guarantee the stability of a household, which requires the presence of other essential factors: recognition from both partners, on an equal basis, of *de facto* rights and duties; *mutual* concessions; a common desire to build something together; and last, but not least, mutual affection. In the absence of these minimum criteria, the marriage will disintegrate.

Polygamy has been practised for centuries. It was known well before the time of Mahomet. But is that sufficient reason to accept it now? If so, should it not be available to both sexes? If we accept this, we must accept all the consequences that this holds for changing the infrastructure of society. Even the system of kinship would have to be reconsidered. Polygamy is a plague which is difficult to combat in Muslim society, where it is deeply entrenched. Whether it is maintained or abolished will depend on women themselves. If we have faith in the possibility of stamping out this oppressive practice, and if we are determined to continue to struggle against it, then victory will be ours. But it will take time.

'The Koran is unalterable. What is written there cannot be challenged. The Koran permits us to take four wives.' This is what we are told by fanatical Muslims or others who are only so in name, and who, under cover of the Islamic religion, practise polygamy and many other things. That, however, is not the problem. What Black African women want is recognition of their identity and their liberty, and respect for their person. This is what African women are demanding. Whatever our number may be today, we will prevail, even if we believe the Malian proverb which says, *'Ni sini do, sini soxomate'*: 'Even if it will happen tomorrow, it will not be tomorrow morning.'

Fodé Diawara, apologist for polygamy

Fodé Diawara is a sociologist and agronomist, of Malian origin, in his 30s, who has studied at university in France. In his book, *Le Manifeste de l'homme primitif*, he undertakes to review and rehabilitate those so-called primitive civilizations which Western civilization, in the name of Reason, has relegated to the stage of 'non-history'. A noble enterprise! A brave step! After all, it is necessary to correct the fallacies about Africa which Westerners and their culture have been responsible for spreading and for maintaining even to the present day. This subject has also been covered by writers like Aimé Césaire (*Discourse on Colonialism*), Franz Fanon (*Black Skin, White Masks* and *The Wretched of the Earth*), Léopold Sédar Senghor, Léon Damas and Cheikh Anta Diop. These writers uncovered a huge ideological and cultural mystification. They shook the foundations of the system accord- ing to which White is superior to Black. This 'civilizing mission' of the West had no further *raison d'être*. The criminals were unmasked. Nothing justified their presence in the colonies. What is more, the very existence of colonies was unacceptable. Their abolition was of prime importance. Colonization and colonial régimes were heading for a downfall.

But what path was taken by these prophets of Black life. According to Hegel's *Reason in History*,

> This continent [Africa] has no interest from the point of view of its own history, but only to show man in a state of barbarism and savagery which prevents him from becoming a part of civilization.

For Hegel Africa is the Dark Continent, shut off since time immemorial from the rest of the world, the land of childhood, 'enclosed before the dawn of conscious history in the black colour of the night'.

So there we have it! Africa is defined and catalogued once and for all. And Hegel's disciples all over the world cry 'Amen!'. In the name of the Concept and of dialectic; let us keep silent.

Hegel also tells us that 'extreme indocility' is a dominant

principle in Africa. And further, that 'In Africa proper, man's development is arrested at the stage of sensory awareness, whence his absolute inability to evolve'.

So, Black women and Black men, what do you make of your 'extreme indocility'? Do you agree to being treated in this fashion in the most docile way possible? In fact, you have no option; it's no fault of yours. You haven't developed beyond the 'stage of sensory awareness'. Hegel *dixit*! And he is not dead: philosophy professors at the Sorbonne use more or less identical terms nowadays.

Having attacked Black Africa (on the basis of what criteria?), Hegel quite confidently goes on to postulate the superiority of Western culture over all others, Europe being essentially the home of 'spiritual unity' of 'the mastery of excess', 'the elevation of the particular to the universal'. Hegel has no compunction in carving out for himself the lion's share of all this. But we can scarcely hold this argument against him, since all he has done is to repeat in his own fashion the arguments of former colonials who settled in Africa in the sixteenth, seventeenth and eighteenth centuries. His view of Africa is already inscribed in an age-old tradition. Did this all begin with the advent of slavery?

In *The Savage Mind*, Claude Levi-Strauss quotes Rousseau approvingly. Rousseau claimed in his *Essai sur l'origine des langues* (II, ch. viii):

One needs to look near at hand if one wants to study men; but to study man one must learn to look from afar; one must first observe differences in order to discover attributes.

Levi-Strauss goes on to warn against the dangers of an analysis which is too ready to assimilate the particular to the universal:

However, it would not be enough to reabsorb particular humanities into a general one. This first enterprise opens the way for others which Rousseau would not have been so ready to accept and which are encumbent on the exact rational sciences: the reintegration of culture into nature and finally of life within the whole of its physio-chemical conditions.

Fodé Diawara's attempt to rehabilitate so-called primitive man is revolutionary, to say the least. As such, we welcome it. Nevertheless, his essay is open to criticism on some scores. For example, let us look at his chapter entitled 'Monogamy, the Original Method of Heterogamous Union, or the Primitive Family'. The chapter begins by attacking the supporters of monogamy:

> A minority of 'intellectuals', of the 'elite' in Black Africa make every effort, in the name of progress, to establish monogamous families, on the bourgeois model. This decision does not come about as the result of their horror of the 'primitive family' (whether based on experience or not) but of the cultural alienation of these 'intellectuals' and the 'elite', which arises from their contact with the West and with Christianity. (*op. cit.* p.193)

Diawara makes no bones about it: for him, the refusal of polygamy is the same thing as cultural alienation. Does that mean that only intellectuals are monogamous in Black Africa? One would have to be totally ignorant of Black Africa, or else be intellectually dishonest, to maintain systematically that every time a couple constitute a monogamous family, it is due to some foreign influence. Certainly, polygamy is a very widespread phemonemon in Black Africa, as is well known. But, at the same time, monogamy is practised not only by intellectuals, but also by a minority of illiterate people.

Does opting for monogamy amount to a systematic negation of one's own culture, of one's own civilization? It would seem so, according to Fodé Diawara, who gives the impression that all monogamists are bowing down before the alleged superiority of the White race. It is not our intention to sit in judgement here on the latter. Our concern is with the role of the Black woman in the context of Black Africa.

In the absence of any concrete eidence, it is easy to give free rein to one's imagination and to express hypotheses about polygamy in Black Africa. Despite speculation on the part of ethnologists, sociologists or anthropologists, there is absolutely nothing which allows us to deduce which came first: monogamous or polygamous families. So let us ask who, here, is holding forth in favour of polygamy? It is no mere coincidence that it happens to be a man. Has he taken the trouble to ask his Black sisters what they think about this? If he had been at all concerned with questions of equality, if he had had any respect for African women, he would have done so. He involves them quite arbitrarily when he says, 'The only evolution of the human family that seems worthy of consideration to me, is when it passes from its original form – based on the monogamous union – to its secondary forms, based on a polygamous or polyandrous union.' (*op. cit.* p.34)

In fact, everything here depends on the expression, 'seems worthy of consideration to me'. In other words, Diawara can only speak in the name of his own subjective values. He seems to start from a definite standpoint: that of the sexual life of Europeans, founded on the monogamous system, evolving towards a timid form of polygamy and a communal existence with the younger generations. This is a curious way of proceeding! His first premise, on which he bases his analysis, is that European society is rapidly degenerating. What have values got to do with this? He gives the impression that polygamy is the sign of a decadent society. Therefore, still going by his logic, we can presume the same phenomenon occurred in Black Africa, which means that polygamy cannot be seen either in terms of its value, or as a result of evolutionary processes.

Is the Black African woman at present in favour of the principle of polyandry? A serious study should be undertaken on this subject, but from my travels in Mali, Guinea, Ivory Coast, Ghana and Nigeria, and from the testimony of the women I have questioned, I have noted an almost unanimous condemnation of the system of polygamy. So, we can deduce that these women would not be in favour of polyandry. Women – particularly in Islamic countries – have, it appears, been conditioned from time immemorial to practice obedience and fidelity towards her one and only husband.

Diawara's faith in polygamy gets the better of his objectivity and the facts suffer, as in the following lines:

In conclusion, while weighty arguments against the mono-gamous bourgeois family are available to everyone, nobody, on the other hand, condemns the 'primitive family' in the name of anything except idealistic rubbish. In the 'primitive group', the relationship between men and women is no longer expressed in terms of equality [Does not that amount to admitting that it was once expressed as such?] . . . Here, the man and the woman constantly and faithfully act out their respective roles in the microcosm of the 'primitive group'. 'Primitive' men and women do not claim equality. (*op. cit*. pp.76-7)

What can the phallocratic Black African man claim, as far as the Black African woman is concerned? An equality of what? Between what? Between whom? Equality in oppression? 'They assume their differences and their complementarity in a collective participation in the economy of the cosmos.' (*op. cit*. p.77) What does their complementarity consist of? Their respective roles? These are the ravings of a madman!

3. Sexual Initiation

A senior woman of Mali: Initiation phase

You want to know who the Malian woman is and what I think of her. I have nothing but the highest opinion of her. She's a fine woman. To give you a picture of her, a description, I have to go back to her early childhood, or at least to her adolescence. In my time, the little Malian girl, whether she was from a village or not, was excised between the age of six and fifteen. That was the first stage of her initiation into the community in which she lived. Once she was healed, she underwent courses of initiation at the age of fifteen or later. The girls were collected into groups to be initiated. They were taught lessons. The first might have as its subject the study of cotton. A lady taught them about the origin and the different uses of cotton. A whole day could be devoted to this. The next day, another old lady would come to talk to them about *karité*, how to treat the plant's fruit to obtain *karité* butter, and about its various uses and functions. There would be lessons on indigo and all the other natural resources that the girls might need to use when they got married. Next, a group of ladies reputed for their wisdom would teach them about marriage, about the life of a couple, about the relationships to be maintained with the in-laws – which in Black Africa can frequently be a source of conflict between husband and wife. These teachers would insist on the respect that the wife must show her husband, on her absolute submission to him, on the fact that she must always be faithful to him. Lessons in child care, maternal and infant welfare were also given. The aim of all this was to make the young initiate into a 'good' wife and mother. The girls would also be given examples from history of women who went to extremes of self-sacrifice, like

Yacine Boubou (the nineteenth-century Senegalese woman who let herself be killed so that her husband could accede to the throne).

The lessons given to the initiates were repeated until all the girls in the group had absorbed them. History, elementary African medicine (the study of plants with curative qualities), natural physical phenomena, such as ageing, physics, astronomy, philosophy (a fatalist philosophy, intended for women), rites – nothing was left out. Everything concerning the everyday, traditional existence of the girl was studied, but always from the point of view of tradition.

In the group of women entrusted with the girls' initiation, there were one or two who were themselves initiates of secret societies. These were women considered to have reached the very highest rung in the ladder of femininity. Their rôle was to tell the girls of the existence of secret societies, and to draw their attention to the fact they should not ever attempt to enter them. Any girl or woman who did not obey their injunctions ran the risk of calling down on herself the curse of the *como*, women's greatest dread. They would not see it, but they would hear it, and death might result. Only those who were themselves initiates of the secret societies could safely see and hear the *como*. All those who gave these lessons had the reputation of being very wise women, but they were also specialists in the subjects they taught and were considered to be models for the girls to emulate. The lessons aimed to prepare girls for conjugal and social life, in other words, for life in the community. The singing lessons given during this initiation bore on marriage, circumcision, excision, baptism, love and the harvest.

When the girls had finished the course of initiation, they were supposed to know what direction their lives would take. They were married either in the same year as their excision and initiation, or a year later. The girls' initiation could last a long time. It could last several months. Generally, it began one or two months after excision. That's how it was in my village.

The education of older girls among the Bambara of Mali

In my village, a father's eldest sister (or in her absence, his youngest sister), nicknamed 'big auntie', plays a very powerful role in the upbringing of his adolescent daughters. In fact, she is entirely responsible for bringing them up. Her training is considered adequate. The girls who are under her authority live with her. They only visit their parents occasionally. When they do go home, they are told of any problems that affect their families. When they go back to 'big auntie', they inform her about such problems, and she then tries to find suitable solutions. She is not obliged to discuss these with her husband or to consult him in any way in these matters.

In view of the fact that older girls in our society must serve as an example to their younger sisters, the old women who initiate them insist on the spirit of sacrifice and resignation that the former must show. It is before excision that the older girls are under the guidance of their 'big auntie'.

On the question of marriage, I will quote you two cases. In both of these cases, the man provides the dowry. Among the Fulani, it comprises eight sheep, a cow and a calf. Among the Bambara, everything is settled in kind.

But nowadays the dowry is fixed by law and is decreased by 25 per cent for a woman who has been married before.

The cattle that the girl acquires through marriage is eventually used to provide dowries for her brothers. In this way, the more cattle obtained for the girl, the more easily her brothers can marry. So there are always more cattle on the women's side than on the men's. Men who are not in a position to marry under these conditions, leave for the towns, or for other countries. So we witness a bigger and bigger exodus from the rural areas, particularly after the years of drought that we have experienced, and emigration to other countries, usually to Europe. The men leave in search of money, so that they will be able to afford, among other things, to marry when they come back.

As for the marriage itself, it is usually 'big auntie' who schemes and manipulates everything. We are very superstitious where I come from. Everyone is very much afraid of big auntie's tears, so much so that often we'll go by what she decides, even against our better judgement.

Before leaving the initiation courses, the girls are told about the different types of men they may come across. The initiators tell them about the 'sheep', that is the gentle, docile husband; the 'monkey', the meddlesome busybody of a husband who is always upsetting his wife, and so on. They also learn how to behave with their husbands' friends, to make sure that a marriage does not end in failure, and how to resist the advances of men who might court them. Initiation is a real school.

Do

I am a Congolese woman, aged 35. I am preparing a sociology thesis. I come from a large family. My father was polygamous; he had three wives. My mother was the third wife. I am the eldest of my mother's children, and the only one to have had any schooling. My father died when I was ten. My mother has two sons and two other daughters, who were born just after me. They helped my mother to look after the house and my two younger brothers. My father was a peasant. I belong to the Bakongo ethnic group, who form the majority of the Congolese. The Bakongo originate from the former kingdom of the Congo, what is now Angola and San Salvador. They form 40 per cent of the population. What strikes me most in respect of the women of the Bakongo people is their sexual initiation. Among Bakongo girls, there is traditionally a certain disgrace in presenting oneself to one's husband as a virgin on the wedding night. Girls should 'prepare' themselves beforehand. This preparation consists of a girl finding some means of losing her virginity. The current method is for her to deflower herself with a cassava tuber. She does this at puberty, from which age girls begin to initiate each other in groups. Here, initiation is not carried out by old women who pass on their knowledge to young adolescent girls.

The Vili

Among the Vili tribe, as far as young girls are concerned, the practice is the exact opposite of the Bakonga. Here, the girl is expected to remain a virgin till the day of her marriage. And the morning after the wedding, the white sheet upon which the marriage has been consummated is exhibited in the presence of the girl's aunts, uncles, and cousins, and every member of her family. It is to the honour of the bride's parents that the girl has preserved her virginity until her marriage. If the girl is not a virgin, tradition demands that her parents pay a fine to the in-laws, and the husband keeps his wife.

Young Vili girls are subjected to the custom of *kikumbi*. This means that once they reach the age of puberty, they are shut up in a little hut. During this period, they are given every kind of little attention. Every day, their bodies are anointed with a mixture of kaolin and a species of dried fruit.

During this period of sequestration, the girls are particularly well fed. Care is taken to make them pleasingly plump, so that they are suitable to become *good* wives. Where I come from, men like their wives to be plump, or fat even – just the opposite of European standards of beauty, according to which a lanky figure is preferred. While she is shut away, the girl must not speak to anyone outside her own family and the women entrusted with looking after her. Usually a hut is built for this purpose in the compound of the girl's parents. Otherwise she will share her mother's room, where a corner will be screened off for her. The end of the sequestration usually coincides with the girl's marriage, which is marked by a series of festivities.

4. Skin Whitening

The 'black' disease of the second half of the twentieth century

> For several years laboratories have been trying to discover a serum for skin-whitening: laboratories have been, quite seriously, rinsing their test-tubes, regulating their balances, and setting up research which would enable the unfortunate Blacks to turn white, and so no longer have to bear the burden of this physical affliction. (Franz Fanon, *Black Skin, White Masks*)

Has the serum for skin whitening finally been discovered? In some circles a link has been made between some products and leukaemia. Be that as it may, soaps and creams are available, which enable Black people to whiten their skins. These seem originally only to have been used for the treatment of acne and seborrhoea. Thus, for example, the product Asepso is known to have curative qualities. But although from a medical point of view these creams and soaps may be very effective against skin rashes, they have the disadvantage that they lighten black skin. Black women use them regularly, even when they do not suffer acne or other skin conditions. Their sole purpose is to lighten their complexions, thinking that this will make them more desirable as sex objects in the Black man's eyes. In fact, a myth has been current for a long time, and still prevails, according to which a light-skinned Black woman is more beautiful than a dark-skinned one. Nothing could be further from the truth. A woman the colour of ebony may of course be a great beauty. Women don't have to play men's game! What is the origin of this myth?

In Jacques Marceau's *Histoire des rites sexuels* (p.312) we find a reference to the light-skinned woman:

> Among the Toma people of Africa who are polygamous, the chiefs have one fetish-wife, chosen for her light complexion. She is marked out from the other wives, because of the respect paid to her (her husband does not beat her), and she is forbidden to work in the house or elsewhere. She is like a mascot and has an almost religious function.

If this light-complexioned wife is a source of happiness for her husband, this is simply because she finds herself in a privileged situation compared to her co-wives who, for their part, are not respected, are beaten, and can be repudiated at any time. In order to preserve this situation, she will seek to please her husband and make him happy. While she is privileged in the attentions she receives, she is also privileged as far as work is concerned. She does absolutely nothing.

Myths are myths, but we are living in a world of reality which has nothing to do with myths. Whitening the skin has become a 'Black' disease in Black African society. As I write, there must be millions of women, Black women, using these skin-lightening creams and soaps on their faces and bodies. The Black woman is denying herself. The Black man too. And everything is encouraging this denial: radio, newspapers, the mass media. In newspapers or magazines designed for Black women, it is not unusual to find whole pages given over to advertisements for these skin-whitening products. For example, there is Ambi, the trade-name of a skin-whitening cream that has cornered the African market and which for some years now has been manufactured in the Ivory Coast. We see photographs of happy couples who have clearly used pounds and pounds of lightening creams and soaps, accompanied by the ludicrous slogan, 'They go... they come... they are noticed. They have the *Ambi chic!*'. Brainwashing! The influence of the show-business world, the consumer society.

What must people in the colonized or neo-colonized and underdeveloped countries do in order to be 'noticed'? Whiten their skin with bleaching agents, instead of arming themselves to develop their countries and find a way out? No! Whiten their skin through mixed marriages? Certainly not! Even in cases where light skin is the result of different races, this takes on an ideological significance. 'Whiten one's offspring' (Whiten one's race) has been the widely admitted principle practised by Black men and women in the Caribbean and in America. The Black populations of these regions were bogged down in the most abject poverty and were obsessed with 'getting out'. They thought that their only way of escape, however illusory this might have been, was to struggle up to the status of the Whites. To what extent was this possible? By working their way up? No. Sons and daughters of transplanted Black slaves were under the thrall of their White masters. The relationship of oppressor to oppressed, which their masters maintained, gave them little opportunity to aspire to the latter's freedom. As slaves, unarmed and transplanted minorities, the Black communities of the Caribbean and America often preferred to stifle their rebellion and suffer in silence, rather than take up arms and fight. So miscegenation, giving birth to children of mixed race, was a means of begetting a new category of people who were more privileged than full-blooded Black people. Miscegenation appeared to be a factor in the social advancement of the Black community. The woman of mixed race frequently tried to marry a White man so that her children would be White, and consequently would belong to the society of the masters, the Whites. This was all the more important since, in that part of the world, the man of colour was thought to be sub-human.

This mixture of races is common in the Caribbean and in Latin America; in both these countries it is the source of conflict, particularly among the female population. Take the case of Columbia, where White women confront women of mixed race and dark-skinned Negresses, accusing both of planning to lure White men away in order to have children by them. This is a divisive factor among women who should be uniting as an oppressed class. What is the aim of this skin-whitening policy? Assimilation? The question remains unanswered. In theory there is no fundamental objection to the physical and cultural mixing of races. But if this were to threaten the survival of a community, be it Jewish or Black, it must be condemned; it is like genocide. In the long run it would amount to the disintegration of Black individuality, and the disappearance of the dark-skinned African.

The whitening of the race by miscegenation is similar in some respects to whitening the skin by the use of bleaching agents. The black colour of the Black is the result of the presence of melanine localized in certain cells of the organism. Similar cells exist in the case of the White races, but the action of melanine in them is inhibited and does not make its presence felt until the skin is exposed to the sun, when it takes on the brown tint of suntan. In Black people, the use of lightening creams and soaps produces desquamation (peeling of the skin) and inhibits the effect of the melanine. The outer layer of black skin peels off and a gradual lightening takes place. The longer these agents are used, the lighter the skin becomes, producing a complexion which resembles that of a person of mixed race, but with an uneven effect. To anyone who knows, a person who has 'lightened' or 'whitened' their skin in this way is easy to spot. Because of the expense, certain Black women who cannot afford a sufficient quantity of these products to 'whiten' the whole body only use them on their faces, so that in less prosperous circles, whitened faces stand out in complete contrast to dark bodies.

These skin-bleaching agents are flooding the markets in America, Africa and Europe. They are on sale in New York, London, Paris, Abidjan and Lagos, to name but a few cities.

What was the aim behind the development of these products? Were the inventors of these bleaching agents indoctrinated with the idea that it was essential to whiten Black people? First 'whiten their brains', then 'whiten their bodies'; next try to find a way of permanently straightening their curly hair, before they endanger the purity of the White race? No answers have appeared yet.

However, what the people who flood the markets with these whitening agents don't tell you is that a whitened skin is a weakened skin. The skin no longer serves as a filter to the sun's rays and is consequently without defences, so it is vulnerable to ulcers and, ultimately, to skin cancer.

Nothing is easier nowadays than for Blacks to turn white, with the help of brainwashing. Measures should be taken against newspapers which publish advertisements for these bleaching agents. They should be boycotted or banned by Black countries. These products should be withdrawn from Black markets. There should be a campaign to spread information about them among Black women as well as men. Let Black women and Black men wear their black colour with dignity and pride. Women must take up the struggle and dispute the arguments for using skin-bleaching agents which are medically recognized as harmful to the organism.

In fact, the only means of eradicating this 'Black' disease of the twentieth century is to raise the consciousness of Black women and men so that they fully accept their identity and over-throw the systems which condone and encourage such practices.

Nowadays, to be a Black woman or a Black man and to retain one's natural complexion is a sign of self-awareness. To be a Black woman or a Black man and to retain one's natural complexion is an act of demystification and demythification. The colour black is not ugly. The colour black is just as good as yellow or white. Criteria for beauty differ from one civilization to another, from one society to another. Everything is relative.

Black people will always be black, whether their skin is whitened or not. So why must they define themselves in relation to others, to Whites for example? Those people who whiten their skins are afraid to stop using these bleaching agents for fear of reverting to their natural black colour – which is in fact what happens. Let them take courage from these words of Aimé Césaire: 'Though the foot of the tree may be painted white, the strength of the bark beneath cries out' (*Et les chiens se taisaient*, p.39), and tell themselves that there is no shame in resuming one's natural colour, any more than there is in retaining one's curly hair.

For the majority of Black women, hair-straightening has also been injurious, often causing loss of hair and in particular burning of the scalp and ears. When a Black woman wears a smooth, straight wig, she is expressing a strong desire – even if an unconscious one – to conform to European aesthetics. Who establishes the criteria of European beauty in Black societies? Certainly not the Black woman. It was the colonial powers. In fact, the Black woman showed herself to be more conservative than the Black man who, alienated and brainwashed by a new ideology, tended more and more to abandon the traditional society in which he had been brought up, turning to the values of a society which was not his own: White society. The Black man thereby confirmed his approval of a White ideal of beauty. Thus the Black woman, when she has reached marrying age, or is already married, conforms, by reacting against her own devalued culture, to the image of the 'other', the White woman, in order to please the Black male. The Black man and the Black woman, far from liberating themselves, thus deepen their own alienation.

Part 3: Feminism and Revolution

While women from industrialized countries are focusing their attention on the problem of creating a typically female language, the daughters of Black Africa are still at the stage of seeking their own dignity, for the recognition of their own specificity as human beings. This specificity has always been refused them by White colonialists or neo-colonialists and by their own Black males. One only needs to glance briefly at history to realize this. Africa in the fifteenth and sixteenth centuries was the source of human merchandise, the 'black gold' of the time: slaves to be scattered all over America and the Caribbean.

It's not a matter of saying, 'Black sisters, look out! The struggle of women from industrialized countries is not our struggle', but simply of reminding ourselves – although some Black women are aware of this – that our own struggle, the Black women's struggle has not yet reached the same point as that of European women. Our primary, fundamental demands are not the same. Institutionalized polygamy flourishes in Black Africa; sexual mutilatory practices flourish, forced marriages, child brides . . . But, on the other hand, Black women have to combat the same scourges as their European sisters. Nevertheless, we must distinguish between two levels of exploitation and oppression of women: the first, where women who are oppressed and exploited do not understand the situation, and remain in thrall, as passive victims – this is the case with a good many Black women, whether traditionalists or not; the second, where exploitation and oppression are partially understood and give rise to theorizing, sometimes leading to movements for the liberation of women, as in the USA and Europe.

But it is essential to clarify certain issues. European feminists have often compared the exploitation of women to that of the

Black people of the USA or Africa. Thus, in the message sent by Kate Millett to the organizers of 'Ten Hours against Rape', held by the MLF (Mouvement pour la Libération des Femmes) at the Mutualité in Paris in June 1976, we read: 'Rape is to women what lynching is to Blacks.' As if it were possible to make the equation: women = Blacks (insofar as both are oppressed) therefore rape = lynching. This is a false argument. Let us compare comparable things. A textual equivalence between 'woman' and 'Black' cannot be justified. One can be of the female sex and of the Black race. If rape is to women what lynching is to Blacks, then what do we make of the rape of Black women by Black men? To get rid of the ambiguity inherent in Kate Millet's words, we must make it clear that she is referring to White women, which she does not do. In which case, the above equation still stands, but still cannot be justified. What, in all this, is the position of the Black woman? European feminists do not seem to know: they continue to satisfy themselves with the false comparison between the situation of Blacks and that of women – by which we must understand White women, even if they don't say so explicitly. Others tell us, 'Women are the Blacks of the human race'. Can they tell us then what or who are Black women? The Blacks of the Blacks of the human race?

You would think that Black women did not exist. In fact, they find themselves denied, in this way, by the very women who claim to be fighting for the liberation of all women.

What emerges from the interviews here is the extent of oppression, exploitation and frustration that is the lot of Black African women. With the exception of a middle-class minority (in this case, a few intellectuals), the Black African woman, be she town-dweller or villager, married, divorced or single, has a deplorable life.

During the colonial period the African woman suffered a double domination, a double enslavement. She was not only subjected to the colonial, but she was also subjected to the colonized African male. After this period, she faced ever greater problems: the aftermath of colonization (decolonization appearing only superficially); the tendency to acculturation. She is still under the yoke of males: father, brother, husband; she is the object of sexual satisfaction on the part of the male and forms part of the proof of his prosperity. In a word, she is both an ornamental symbol and a maid-of-all-work.

Let us return to the colonial period. Surely the true status of Black African women was identical to that of the Afro-American or Caribbean woman in the days of slavery. She, like them had to comply with the sexual whims of her White master who, having appropriated her lands, had become omnipotent in her very home.

We are not concerned here with the problem of the liberation of Black women in terms of priorities, because two aspects of the Black African woman's struggle are closely linked: the struggle for effective economic and political independence and the struggle for the recognition of and respect for the rights and duties of men and women of all races.

The one must not exclude the other. Ideally both struggles should be waged simultaneously. 'That doesn't seem possible,' would be the reply of sexists and racists. To which we shall retort: we are in Africa, with all that this entails (a colonial or neo-colonial society, patriarchy, feudalism). In Algeria, Guinea-Bissau and many other countries which have fought wars for national liberation, genuinely aiming to free their people, including women, we find that there has been no liberation for the latter. In Algeria, women still wear the veil and are confined to the traditional tasks of servant, childbearer and housekeeper. On top of these, she has the not inconsiderable role of preserving traditions and customs, which are either too rigid for change or have not yet been adapted to our times.

Women must certainly achieve total independence, but they will have to fight for it, they will have to wrest it from society. They will have to call men's bluff and prove their independence; they will have to reject the alienating influences which have cast a shadow over their lives in the past, and still do to this day.

They have not only to wage a class war but also a sex war. The American Shulamith Firestone has fully understood the complexity and diverse nature of women's struggles. 'We shall need a sexual revolution', she states, 'much larger than – inclusive of – a socialist one to truly eradicate all class systems.' (*The Dialectic of Sex. The Case for Feminist Revolution*, p.20)

Black African Women

In the former colonies, be they French, Belgian, or other, the situation of the Black woman today is the same as that of her sisters in Zimbabwe or Latin America. Like her Black brother, she suffers from the damaging aftermath of colonialism and the crimes of the colonials. But her sufferings are greater than those of men, for she is not only faced with White racism, the exploitation of her race by the colonial, but also the domination that men, Black as well as White, exercise over her, by virtue of the patriarchal system in which both live.

Because she is a colonized person, she is obliged to work for the colonial, just as the Black male is. She is exploited as a unit of production. What is more, she is the cheapest form of labour for the colonial, by virtue of both her colour and her sex. Badly paid by the colonial, she is also underpaid in comparison with men. Therefore she is exploited not only as a Black, but also because she is a woman. But which of these comes first? The fact of being Black, without regard to her sex, makes her the slave of the colonial who simply regards her as a beast of burden in the same way as her Black brother. But the difference between them is soon established. It is possible that it was present before the colonial arrived, but it is just as likely that he introduced it to the land that he 'confiscated', seeing that this arrangement characterizes his own society, where women are also undervalued.

Both colonial and patriarchal systems decree that the Black woman's work is worth less than that of the Black male. This is translated into concrete terms in the wage structure, in the importance attached to her, as well as in every other field. Her value as a commodity only goes up for the colonist when he sees her as an object of sexual satisfaction. (And how!)

It is as well to remember that the submissiveness of the Black female lies behind these communities of half-castes which developed in the colonies. As long as she – the female – is under the domination of the colonial – the male – her relationship to him will always be that of victim to victimizer. He is invested with the power to commit psychological and actual rape on the colonized group.

By virtue of her sexual role, the Black woman is sometimes

regarded by the White man as a woman. In other words, she is considered to be a woman without being essentially human. Difficult to conceive! We are not far from the old Catholic concept, according to which women have no souls.

Wherever the colonials have passed through they have left their mark, not only at the political level, but also economically and in society generally: the institution of colonial and neo-colonial régimes, the imposition of monocultures, as in Senegal, where the majority of agricultural land is given over to the cultivation of groundnuts, to the detriment of other food crops. This is an evil which Aimé Césaire denounces so eloquently when anyone speaks to him of the progress achieved by the colonial:

> They talk to me of progress, of 'achievements', diseases cured, improved standards of living.
>
> *I* am talking about societies drained of their essence, cultures trampled underfoot, institutions undermined, lands confiscated, religions smashed, magnificent artistic creations destroyed, extraordinary *possibilities* wiped out. (*Discourse on Colonialism*, p.21).

In addition to this, we should remember the emergence of a half-caste population, however small. Raped by the colonial, or seduced thanks to some trickery, the Black woman is reduced to the degrading status of an object of pleasure. With her essence denied, what remains of her self? *There is nothing of her left;* or rather, she is reduced to the state of an instrument. In such a context can there be any love between the colonial and the colonized woman? Or can any human relationship be possible?

The object of this discussion is not to state whether this relationship is possible, but to expose the different forms of oppression and exploitation suffered by the Black woman at the hands of the male colonist. We have finally to consider the relationship of the Black woman to the Black male: if the latter is the slave of the colonist, she is the slave of a slave.

The situation of the Black woman in an African colonized state is not identical to that of her coloured sister in Latin America. The point where they differ is in their relationship to the Whites. In the African colony, the White man is an intruder, an invader;

although he is numerically in the minority, he is nevertheless in a position of strength. In Latin America, the Black woman has been transplanted, and here she is in the minority. She belongs to the slave race, imported from Black Africa and herded into the plantations as labour in the cultivation of cocoa and coffee. The Blacks of Latin America are not only outnumbered but also outbalanced in military strength. They are unarmed, therefore more effectively controlled by the Whites. And this makes the Black woman, belonging as she does to the most deprived social and racial group, the victim of a double oppression.

To sum up: she is exploited by virtue of her sex; her wages even undercut the low wage of the Latin American Black male. Moreover, outside her own community she has no contact with other social classes, unless she marries a White man or goes in for prostitution. In this respect, the situation of the Black women of Latin America is similar to that described by Franz Fanon in *Black Skin, White Masks*.

How should the colonial or neo-colonial context in which the Black African woman lives affect our understanding of a feminist movement aiming to challenge her status in society? Challenging the status of women amounts to challenging the structures of an entire society when this society is patriarchal in nature. All the problems of society – political, cultural, economic – are inextricably linked to the problem of women. The problem of women belongs in a general context.

Where the European woman complains of being doubly oppressed, the Black woman of Africa suffers a threefold oppression: by virtue of her sex, she is dominated by man in a patriarchal society; by virtue of her class she is at the mercy of capitalist exploitation; by virtue of her race she suffers from the appropriation of her country by colonial or neo-colonial powers. Sexism, racism, class division; three plagues! In order to succeed, the Black African feminist movement must set its sights on eradicating these three plagues from society. In other words, the Black African women's struggle cannot find a place in any scheme which denies the specificity of women's problems and which only sees their solution in a struggle for national liberation, like that of Algeria. We cannot repeat often enough: Algerian women participated in Algeria's struggle for national liberation. But Algerian women have not been liberated!

Who can guarantee that a war of liberation in a Black African country would in fact lead to the suppression of clitoridectomy, of infibulation? Black African women can – and must – no longer allow men to decide for them and to manipulate their lives.

No system of social life has ever, on any level, been able to function without the effective participation of women. They are relied on to bring up children and look after the home, and to perform all the attendant soul-destroying, thankless and repetitive tasks. As for the man, the job that he appropriates, earning the daily bread, is far and away more profitable than the woman's tasks. His place in the bosom of society is much more interesting. It gives him access to the world at large, the opportunity to develop his intellectual and physical faculties in a range of experiences.

The image of the woman as object is found in all societies at all levels. In industrialized societies, the immigrant – man or woman – is made aware of this state of affairs by observing both public and private life, notably the nuclear family.

According to phallocratic logic the situation is quite natural, so the question whether all that is posited as 'feminine' really is so never arises. What is more normal in a society where the male reigns supreme? Whether they come from colonized countries or not, phallocrats are all alike and exercise the same oppression over women. How can we put an end to such a situation?

Women are beginning to realize the need to fight against a system which denies women an authentic existence – that system which is patriarchal and phallocratic. Traditionalism and revolution clash against each other: there is an endless succession of advances and retreats, of rebellions and repression, of short-lived victories and temporary setbacks.

Sometimes the workers triumph, but their triumph is brief. The real outcome of their struggles is less the immediate success than the growing solidarity of the workers. To struggle means to fight with resolution and faith in the certainty of victory, in the promise of future happiness for ourselves or for others; to fight with the firm conviction that positive success will ensue – whether we live to see it or not. We must fight on.

Colonized or neo-colonized peoples are living in a dilemma: whether to revolt against a system which exploits them, or passively to accept slavery. Either way, the colonized people 'get it in the neck'. In the first place, the indigenous population suffers the intrusive, oppressive presence of the 'settlers' – a presence which they experience as aggression. These settlers subject them to a savage exploitation which is underlined by an attempt to dehumanize them. The circumstances of the indigenous people are inevitably affected: customs are disrupted, lives upset, social structures shattered. The colonized native may not and cannot behave as a free person; he or she must live and act according to the disposition of the settler. This state of affairs dehumanizes the inhabitants. Their liberty is alienated, they are reduced to the state of an instrument. The settler makes use of them, and when they no longer serve a useful purpose or when, in the colonial context, they become a nuisance, the settler disposes of them. This 'nuisance' may well indicate an attempt to stand up to the settler, a refusal to obey which unleashes the forces of repression. The rebel is truck down like a mad dog. That is not an infrequent occurrence: let us not forget Algeria, Vietnam – and it is still going on in South Africa.

Early in 1976, French television offered us the shameful spectacle of a White South African family amusing themselves at the expense of a group of unarmed Blacks walking past carrying bundles on their heads. The White man shot at them, causing his wife and children to laugh hysterically. They laughed and laughed at this mock assassination of Blacks. They laughed till they cried at the sight of the victims of this cruel sport making off as fast as their legs could carry them. But we'll see who has the last laugh. An alternative strategy lies open to the colonized: while some are sunk in passive submission, others revolt. They take up arms, slave confronts master. The television programme to which we have just referred ended with the announcement of the death of the sadistic, murderous settler. He stepped on a landmine. History is rich in examples of similar violent retribution: Dien bien Phu, Algeria, and more recently, Guinea-Bissau, Vietnam, and Angola are outstanding examples.

Man, the enemy of woman?

Some women tend to equate man with society and by inference see men as their principal enemy. We do not feel that, as far as Black Africa is concerned, men are the enemy. It is certainly true that in any patriarchal system institutions are set up by men, and this might reinforce the arguments given by 'sexist' feminists; but we should ask ourselves whether or not men are alienated as well. Doesn't the very fact of having devised a system of values which disadvantage women offer clear proof of men's alienation? The oppression to which he subjects women, and which he perceives as something quite natural, is justified according to an idea of 'complementarity'. In a patriarchal society, man himself is alienated, so he is not free either. The sex which oppresses the other is not a free sex. A society made up of non-alienated individuals would be an egalitarian society, in which there would be neither master nor slave, neither tyrant nor tyrannized, neither colonial nor colonized, neither chief nor subordinate.

Such a society does not exist. Up until now there have only been attempts to create it. It is now our task to do so. To succeed in this, sexism must be excluded from our praxis, from the praxis of every woman enlisted in the struggle.

A tribute to our mothers

What can we say about customs, civilization, culture? How do we stand in respect of these? Is it our responsibility to ensure their survival? Or should we condemn them as decadent? There is no doubt that they are the defining characteristics of a race. But no culture is static, any more than a civilization is; so customs too must change for better or for worse.

Do Black Africans follow Europeans in considering their customs barbarous? How are they preserved? How were they established? A relationship exists between the myths and customs of Black Africa. Does this mean that they determine each other? It is difficult to find the answers to these questions owing to the paucity of unbiased documentation. Most of the available infor-

mation comes from colonials, who were often eager to document
the different ethnic groups with whom they came into contact.
We hear from ethnologists, anthropologists, sociologists, or simply civil servants. The last were not concerned with recording
African customs objectively and indeed did not take the trouble
to understand their real significance within the indigenous societies. Unbiased studies on Black Africa, written by Whites in the
colonial period, are few and far between.

Colonial logic aimed at undermining the structure of traditional Black African societies and the destruction of the Black
identity. Their civilization was, if not destroyed, at least seriously
damaged by colonization. This is what Jean-Paul Sartre is referring to when he says,

> The command goes out to relegate the inhabitants of the
> annexed territory to the level of the ape, to justify the settler
> in treating them like beasts of burden. Colonial violence not
> only aims to keep these subjected people at arm's length, but
> it also seeks to dehumanize them. No effort will be spared to
> break up their traditions, to substitute our language for
> theirs, to *destroy their cultures* [author's italics] without
> offering them our own; they will be stupefied by work.
> (*Situations V. Colonialism and neo-colonialism*)

However, some things have survived in spite of this, especially
in ritual and cultual matters. The crimes committed by Europeans did not succeed in wiping out the entire Black African civilization, for certain typically African customs have survived.
This was no accident, but the result of continual resistance to
their erosion, as for example in the matter of initiation rites
which have remained virtually unchanged for centuries in Black
Africa, right up to the present day. What is the reason for this?
Capitulation on the part of Black Africans features in practically
every field during the colonial period. But it was women in particular who took it upon themselves to preserve certain customs. We
should pay them tribute. It is because our mothers, our elders,
had the charge of children that they were — and remain — responsible for training them, for transmitting certain myths and beliefs,
and instilling in them a spirit of submission to customs. In refus-

ing to allow **Black African** civilization to be destroyed, our mothers were revolutionary. Yet some people describe this attitude as conservative. These women felt the need to preserve something that was precious to them – their cultural heritage. They became aware of something urgent that needed to be done; something had to be saved – that something which was indispensable to the preservation of the Black African as such: the Black African civilization. This was their aim, and in this they succeeded by dint of insisting on maintaining ancestral practices. Although they did not challenge their state of bondage to men, we nevertheless pay tribute to these women.

BLACK WOMAN
The Black woman is not simply
COLOUR
The Black woman is not simply
FLESH
The Black woman is not simply
MOTHER
The Black woman is not simply
LOVER
The Black woman is not simply
MUSE
The Black woman is not simply . . .
Praised in song as lover, loving-flesh,
praised in song as mother, 'mother-protection'
praised in song as colour, 'colour-affirmation'
the songs about the Black woman
do not say
who IS
the Black woman.
These songs say little
of her afflictions,
pain or pleasure,
heartbreaks, hopes,
. . . her LIFE
The Black woman
'That thing lives'

The Black woman,
Woman, 'that thing' lives woman
'That thing' lives that thing
with battles
    setbacks
    victories
Woman, Black woman, Productive force, Matrix, Fighter.
'That thing' IS
The Black woman IS

Negro-African women, women of the Third World, women of the industrialized countries, the same fight!

The emancipation of women must go hand in hand with men's relinquishing of a feudal and bourgeois way of thinking. As for women themselves, they would be wrong to wait for government and party directives to bring them freedom; they would do better to count on no-one but themselves and to fight. (Ho Chi Minh)

Women, there is a common denominator in your lives: phallocratic violence. It is this violence which makes you think that you don't amount to anything on your own, without the other, the one who has got 'something between his legs', the one with the phallus. It is this violence which tries by every possible means to make you play second fiddle. It is this violence of expression which sometimes robs you of your self-possession, only to bring you face to face with your true self, however debilitated and battered by male phallocratic behaviour: your noble, dignified, true self that men seek to alienate or destroy. This insidious, misogynous violence can, like a monster, present itself in different disguises. It can take on a deceptive appearance to beguile you, to throw dust in your eyes; then may come your violent awakening, or you may be harassed or even murdered in your blind, charmed sleep. This violence is the daily lot of all oppressed women throughout the world, whatever they may do. Illiterate or intellectual, none of them escape. It is not a metaphysical violence; it is real and concrete. It can be not only brutal but also subtle. However, this male violence remains, as distinct from revolutionary violence, the violence of a system of slavery, which desires the domination of the other, the woman. In this sense, it can be considered a form of terrorism.

Whatever form it may take, this violence results in the destruction of the human being. It has a name: phallocratic fascism. As such it must be totally eliminated from every society, from every social class.

Nevertheless, many people have doubts about the common nature of the struggles waged by Black African women, women of the Third World and women from Europe. How could these struggles be identical, in view of the different industrial development, different material and cultural conditions?

What are the specific problems faced by European women? In spite of the level of development reached by their societies, they still feel oppressed and exploited by men. Is this oppression of European women identical to that of the workers? We maintain that there is no common measure between the exploitation of the worker and that suffered by women.

Let us explain. The working woman suffers from the same oppression and exploitation by the capitalist system as the male worker, but to a greater degree since the woman's work is often under-rated. Irrespective of this, the woman, compared with the man – her husband, partner, brother or father – suffers from another form of exploitation which stems from her subjection to the patriarchal system.

How do the problems faced by women in Black Africa compare, and how have women there responded to them? In particular, what is their position regarding feminist movements?

Black African women, whether feminist or not, have participated in the national struggles waged on their own soil, thus proving themselves well aware of the problems faced by their countries and their societies. At the present time, we see an increase in the number of women involved in the liberation movements of their countries. Even if Black women were not the instigators of these struggles (and that still remains to be proved), whenever it has been a question of fighting to free their countries from a colonial or neo-colonial yoke, they have hastened to throw in their lot with the men. Then and only then do we see any sort of equality between men and women. They fight together, literally bearing arms for a common ideal: the liberation of their country. On the field of battle, women run the same risks as men. Whether they belong to an underground resistance movement or not, the colonial perceives them as a target just as much as he does the man. Such a situation puts them on an equal footing: mother fighting side by side with father; girl with boy. The man is forced to recognize the equal status of woman. It is no longer a question of asking whether she is not too weak or too stupid to know how to pull a trigger or throw a hand grenade at the right moment, or hide something or other in the right place. A woman is just as capable of assimilating the techniques of guerrilla warfare as a man. Tasks on the battlefield are shared without distinction according to sex.

But what is the position as soon as the war is over, the victory obtained? This is a logical, legitimate question to ask, since the world has seen the end of several wars of liberation in recent years. Once these wars are over, 'things return to normal'. In other words, men resume their former occupations, and so do women. The latter have not managed to eliminate certain contradictions inherent in the patriarchal society to which they belong, nor to rise above them. They have not yet succeeded in getting rid of customs which have no strategic value (tatooing, wearing the veil, etc.). We must refute the claim that the preservation of those customs today is our way of resisting the ever-increasing power of neo-colonialism or imperialism.

Guinea

Guinea obtained its independence in 1958, as a consequence of its rejection of de Gaulle's proposed new constitution. A socialist republic was immediately declared. This choice was to have important repercussions for the Guinean masses, imposing gigantic pressures on them. But what happened to the Guinean woman? Where does she now stand in the new order?

We get the impression that, in its daily life – as was reflected in the collective interview reported in an earlier chapter – Guinea is in a state of evolution, while still bearing the deep imprint of its cultural past. Ancestral values die hard. And in certain places and some circles they hold sway. However, it must be emphasized that Guinea is one of the countries that included the integration of women in its political programme. It is one of the first States to promote a policy of integration *and* emancipation of women.

When it was necessary to oppose the reactionary forces which sought to keep Guinea under colonial domination, the women of Guinea armed themselves and took their place in the forefront of the fight against the enemy. We can quote the example of the heroic M'Balia Camara who was assassinated on 9 February 1955, disembowelled while she was carrying the child of the colonials' puppet of that period, David Sylla. The date of her death is celebrated as the National Day of Guinean Women. Guinea also has the highest rate of female participation in government of any African state. By way of comparison, in 1977 Algeria had eight women deputies out of a total of 261; while in Guinea 22 of its 72 deputies were women. Similarly, a woman, Mme Mafory Bangoura, who had never attended a French school, was appointed Minister for Social Affairs and leader of the women's section of the PDG (Parti Démocratique de Guinée). It is also noteworthy that Guinea's representative at the United Nations is a woman. Women are to be found in every sector of public life. They are engineers, pharmaceutical chemists, secondary and university teachers, regional governors, heads of ministerial cabinets, directors of business concerns. This shows concern for women's progress – but it's not the only sign of this concern.

A genuine desire for change is perceptible among the people of Guinea. This is why we must try to understand (though not to justify or excuse) some of the fundamental consequences of this desire. Change, if it does not come about as a result of long-term reforms, is of necessity sudden and brutal; it is change through revolution. We must recognize this before evaluating what is being and has been achieved by the present Guinean régime.

There has been a great deal of talk of 'fabricated' plots and assassinations in Guinea. Some people claim that it has a dictatorial régime. Not being in a position to judge it objectively, we do not intend to indict the internal politics of the country. We must however admit that the condition of women there is far superior to that of any other African state.

The first president of the Republic of Guinea, Ahmed Sékou Touré, seemed to give priority to the task of raising the consciousness of the masses and giving them an education relevant to their needs and social structures, before worrying about other problems. He must have been among those who say, 'He who forms youth is master of the future'.

What is more, having rejected colonization and all forms of imperialism, Guinea was increasingly cut off from industrialized countries, although relations have recently been re-established. Is Guinea a progressive country? Its motto seems to be, 'Dignity in poverty rather than slavery with opulence'. But is it blinkered to look only at the positive aspects of this country? In spite of claiming to be progressive, is it not in many respects archaic? We are thinking primarily of the continued practice of excision, to which 85 per cent of our Guinean sisters are subjected. To quote the following statistics from P. Hanry's *Erotisme africaine* (pp.47-8):

> 84 per cent of the girls are excised, with only 8 per cent stating that they are not. Only a very small percentage of women protest against their fate: 12 per cent deplore their own excision and 35 per cent declare that they do not intend to have their daughters excised. This last figure, higher than the preceding one, certainly implies a protest, but we must compare it with the 44 per cent who will have their daughters excised and the 21 per cent who have no opinion at present but who risk giving way to the call of tradition when the time arises.

Are we saying then, that various political considerations and analyses have deliberately disregarded women's problems? Or were those responsible unaware of their existence? An objective historical analysis would show these practices up for what they are – an attack on women themselves – and not disguise them, or support them on the pretext that they form a part of the traditional cultural past, which is to be held sacred.

Polygamy, too, is among the conditions which restrict the lives of Guinean women – although the country is ahead of other West African states on this count; a struggle against it has been under way since 1968. Indeed on 16 February 1974 Sékou Touré declared, 'We must create a hatred of polygamy among the rising generation'.

Conclusion: What Suggestions Should We Make to Our Black Sisters?

It is a great encouragement to us to know that the Black women's struggle does not date from today. In days gone by our ancestors fought with whatever means they had to hand. At a time when contraception was unknown, some of the women deported to the Caribbean killed their infant children by piercing their skulls with a needle or a thorn, rather than let them live to suffer slavery.

Should they be condemned? They might have committed suicide, you may retort, rather than kill their children. But the important thing for them was to fight on: the fight against slavery meant wresting as many victims as possible from the hands of the White masters.

But what suggestions should we make to Black women nowadays? Should their aim be a society similar to that of Europe, which is fast falling to pieces? Must Africa adopt this as a model? If anything can be done to save a state newly emerged from the claws of the colonials, or still controlled by the latter, it is certainly not by imitating a society which has seen the collapse of the family and the reign of individualism. You are not unaware of the importance of the family in Black Africa – the extended family, including grandparents, parents, near relatives and children. We wish to live a genuine, decent, whole and enhancing life, in community. The struggle of the Black African woman can and must be conceived in some other way than as a carbon copy of the European woman's struggle. First of all, the forms of existence are different: Europe is industrialized, whereas Black Africa is not; lifestyles and family arrangements are incompatible. There can therefore be no question of superimposing the social structures of the West onto Black Africa.

But, note well! As women we feel solidarity with the Italian girl who was raped by her brother when she was sixteen, and wished for an abortion which the doctors refused her – the case which was widely reported in 1977. We feel solidarity with all women political prisoners, like Angela Davies and Eva Forest, wherever they come from, and all the women of Vietnam who fought bravely to guarantee a victory over the American 'paper tigers', and with the Black African women who took part in the war of liberation in Zimbabwe.

It has long been thought that the Black is rather like the ape, incapable of any initiative (their spirit in truth having been damaged by the colonials), incapable of adopting an original stance towards the world. When a Black woman manifests her solidarity with women of other races in some concrete fashion, she does so out of a deep conviction, not simply to imitate their practices as certain traditionalist Blacks maintain. Those who think their behaviour is imitative are clearly unaware of the magnitude of the female problem, or else are motivated by a systematic desire to divide women. Solidarity among women must be understood to mean that all women – irrespective of race or class, be they Black, Yellow or White, hardworking housewives or middle-class employees, non-proletarian or *lumpen proletariat* – are exploited by the patriarchal system.

By affirming her solidarity with other women's struggles, the Black woman forms part of a sisterhood. Just as Aimé Césaire says, 'whenever a single miserable wretch is lynched, one miserable man tortured anywhere in the world, so I too am mob-murdered, maltreated.' (*Et les chiens se taisaient*) We must echo his words, saying that whenever and wherever any female person is excised, infibulated, mutilated, beaten or slandered, this is an attack on ourselves.

As women, we offer ourselves as the sisters of all oppressed women. Whether this sisterhood is accepted or not, it is there. It is offered. Those women to whom it is offered will do with it what they will. We mark ourselves off from that inferiority complex to which Aimé Césaire refers in his *Discourse on Colonialism*, from the 'millions of men in whom fear has been cunningly instilled, who have been taught to have an inferiority complex, to tremble, kneel, despair and behave like flunkeys' (*op. cit.* p.22).

We are beginning to assume our own identity. No matter what the opinion is of the other: the White person. The Black woman does not have to define herself in comparison with the other, the White woman, any more than the Black man has to in relation with the White man. The first indication of an understanding of this is that Africans in urban circles are becoming aware of an African existence expressed in thoughts and actions which have broken with the colonial or neo-colonial ideology. A return to our roots has been set in motion; credit is given once more to certain usages, for example to wearing typically African clothing and coiffures. This resists the process which encouraged Black women to identify with Whites, and which is revealed in such actions as permanently straightening frizzy hair or wearing of smooth-haired wigs on an ebony skin, 365 days out of 365!

African canons of beauty are by no means identical to those of other races, and as such they form a part of the specificity of Black culture. When the Black man defines his ideal of beauty according to one which is foreign to his society, the Black woman is caught in a trap; she makes the mistake of playing the game into which the Black man forces her. She betrays herself, denies herself, and what is more she betrays her civilization and her race.

We read in Franz Fanon's *Black Skin, White Masks* that a Black man who was accused of having sexual relations with a White woman was liable to the penalty of castration, while a White man who raped a Black woman incurred no penalty, not even a reprimand. It is thereby the duty of Black women to fight with determination against a system which institutionalizes injustice.

It is easy to understand what Simone de Beauvoir refers to in *The Second Sex*, when she talks about the difficulty of establishing a genuine solidarity based on gender, across the barriers of colour and class: 'Middle-class women', she claims, 'feel solidarity with middle-class men, and not with working-class women; White women with White men, not with Black women.' That does give expression to the general tendency. It is true that some effective solidarity does exist between Black and White women; but it is only to be found among a small minority i.e. feminists. (If then!) And we are not talking about those militants who reckon that they can show their solidarity with other women by being subservient towards them. The last thing that such an attitude can achieve is the liberation of women.

In the past our ancestors were deported to America and the Caribbean to cultivate the plantations for the White man. They lived in servitude. Those who were lucky enough to remain in their own land were also subjected to servitude. This state of affairs continues to this day, although in a more subtle form. It is revealed when any White person, male or female, makes use of any Black person, male or female; to satisfy their curiosity, benefit by our services and then say, 'Thank you very much! We don't know you any more!'.

This is the kind of relationship which held sway between colonial ancestors of the Whites and our colonized or enslaved ancestors. We can no longer tolerate this situation. The Black woman, the Black man, no longer have to be puppets. Every Black woman, every Black man must expel the zombie which slumbers within them, however painful such a process may be.

It may seem disconcerting or suspicious that women keep silent about their hardships. Disconcerting inasmuch as it seems to indicate that they are unaware of suffering any victimization or oppression. Suspicious in the sense that, far from being unaware, some women might derive a certain satisfaction from their situation, or at least prefer to give that impression. In either case, the solution to women's problems is not close at hand.

So what should be done? It is of primary importance that women regroup, break away from any mixed organizations inherently fascistic in structure and dominated by a phallocratic ideology. They must bear in mind that the effective liberation of any oppressed masses involves a struggle both with and against women, with and against men. In fact the solution to women's problems must be collective and international. This is the only way effectively to change their status. We must remember that the history of the condition of women has not been a static one. But the rate of progress gives the impression that those who are fighting for their own liberation and that of their societies are embarked on a long-term struggle. It is not a race for the sprinter but for the long-distance runner. Let women equip themselves to win this race.

Paris 5 July 1977

Bibliography

Simone de Beauvoir, *The Second Sex*, trans. H.M. Parshley, London: Jonathan Cape, 1953, reprinted 1972; *The Woman Destroyed*, trans. Patrick O'Brian, London: Collins, 1969.

Abdelwahab Boudhiba, *La Sexualité en Islam*, Paris: PUF, 1975.

Bulletin de la Société Médicale d'Afrique Noire, 1975, Vol. XX, No. 3.

Aimé Césaire, *Discourse on Colonialism*, trans. Joan Pinkham, New York/London: Monthly Review Press, 1972; *Et les chiens se taisaient*, Paris: Présence Africaine, 1956; *Return to My Native Land*, trans. J. Berger and A. Bostok, Harmondsworth: Penguin, 1969.

Phyllis Chesler, *Women and Madness*, New York: Doubleday, 1972.

Angela Davis, *An Autobiography*, London: Hutchinson, 1975.

Fodé Diawara, *Le manifeste de l'homme primitif*, Paris: Grasset, 1972.

Franz Fanon, *Black Skin, White Masks*, trans. C.L. Markman, New York/London: Paladin, 1970; *The Wretched of the Earth*, trans. Constance Farrington, London: MacGibbon & Kee, 1965.

Shulamith Firestone, *The Dialectic of Sex: The Case for Feminist Revolution*, London: The Women's Press, 1979.

Betty Friedan, *The Feminist Mystique*, London: Gollancz, 1965.

Marcel Griaule, *Dieu d'eau: Conversations with Ogotemmêli: An Introduction to Dogon Religious Ideas*, London: International African Instititute, 1965.

Benoîte Groult, *Ainsi soit-elle*, Paris: Grasset, 1975; *La part des choses*, Paris: Grasset, 1972.

Pierre Hanry, *Erotisme africain*, Paris: Payot, 1970.

Ibrahima Baba Kake, *Anne Zingha*, Paris: 1975.

Jomo Kenyatta, *Facing Mount Kenya: The Tribal Life of the Kikuyu*, London: Secker & Warburg, 1953.

Jacques Lantier, *La Cité magique et magie en Afrique noire*, Paris: Arthème Fayard, 1972.

Jean Laude, *The Arts of Black Africa*, trans. J. Decock, Berkeley: University of California Press, 1971.

Claude Lévi-Strauss, *The Savage Mind*, London: Weidenfeld & Nicolson, 1966.

Mamadou Madeira-Keïta, 'Aperçu sommaire sur les raisons de la polygamie chez les Malinké', in *Etudes guinéennes*, No. 4, Conakry, 1950.

J. Marcireau, *Histoire des rites sexuels*, Paris: Laffont, 1971.

Denise Paulme, *Classes d'age en Afrique de l'Ouest*, Paris: Plon, 1971.

Erin Pizzey, *Scream Quietly or the Neighbours Will Hear*, London: Penguin, 1974.

Ahmad Abd Ar Raziq, *La Femme au temps des Mamelouks en Egypte*, Cairo: Institut Française d'Archéologie Orientale, 1973.

Wilhelm Reich, *The Sexual Revolution*, trans. T.P. Wolfe, London: Vision Press, 1969.

Sheila Rowbotham, *Women, Resistance and Revolution*, London: Penguin, 1974.

Pierre Samuel, *Amazones, guerrières et gaillardes*, Grenoble: Presses Universitaires de Grenoble, Collection Actualités et Recherches, 1975.

Jean-Paul Sartre, *Situations V Colonialisme et néo-colonialisme*, Paris: Gallimard, 1964.

Jean Suret-Canale, 'La Femme dans la société africaine', in *La Vie Africaine*, No. 56, Paris, 1965.

Annie de Villeneuve, 'Etude sur une coutume somalie: les Femmes Cousues', *Journal de la société des africanistes*, Paris: 1937.